I0015114

Amazing Arduino special projects like Air quality, Auto pet Feeder, Alcohol Detector, Gyro sense etc..,

Amazing Arduino special projects like Auto pet Feeder, Alcohol Detector, Gyro sense etc..,

CONTENTS

CONTENTS

ACKNOWLEDGMENTS

The writer might want to recognize the diligent work of the article group in assembling this book. He might likewise want to recognize the diligent work of the Raspberry Pi Foundation and the Arduino bunch for assembling items and networks that help to make the Internet of Things increasingly open to the overall population. Yahoo for the democratization of innovation!

INTRODUCTION

The Internet of Things (IOT) is a perplexing idea comprised of numerous PCs and numerous correspondence ways. Some IOT gadgets are associated with the Internet and some are most certainly not. Some IOT gadgets structure swarms that convey among themselves. Some are intended for a solitary reason, while some are increasingly universally useful PCs. This book is intended to demonstrate to you the IOT from the back to front. By structure IOT gadgets, the per user will comprehend the essential ideas and will almost certainly develop utilizing the rudiments to make his or her very own IOT applications. These included ventures will tell the per user the best way to assemble their very own IOT ventures and to develop the models appeared. The significance of Computer Security in IOT gadgets is additionally talked about and different systems for protecting the IOT from unapproved clients or programmers. The most significant takeaway from this book is in structure the tasks yourself.

1.TVOC AND CO2 MEASUREMENT USING ARDUINO AND CCS811 AIR QUALITY SENSOR

"Tragically, for the benefit of advancement, we have contaminated the air, water, soil and the nourishment we eat". So checking the air quality is critical now days in view of contamination. For structuring an air quality checking framework we need solid and dependable air quality sensor. Despite the fact that there are many Air Quality parameters yet the most significant are CO2 and TVOC. So for detecting CO2 as well as TVOC, we are utilizing CCS811 Air Quality Sensor.

In this instructional exercise, we are demonstrating that how to detect TVOC and CO2 utilizing CCS811 air quality sensor with Arduino. Likewise, you will figure out how to interface CSS811 with Arduino.

Material Required

- CCS811 Air Quality Sensor
- Arduino UNO
- LCD 16*2

- Potentiometer (10k)
- Connecting Wires
- Breadboard

Circuit Diagram

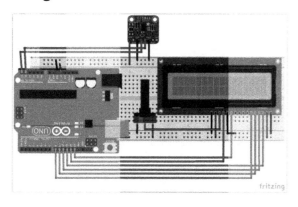

CCS811 Air Quality Sensor

CCS811 Air Quality Sensor is a ultra-low control computerized gas sensor which incorporates a MOX (metal oxide) gas sensor to recognize a wide scope of VOCs (Volatile Organic Compounds) for indoor air quality observing with a coordinated MCU. MCU comprises of ADC as well as I2C interface. It depends on an ams one of a kind smaller scale hotplate innovation which enables profoundly solid answers for Gas Sensors, with low control utilization.

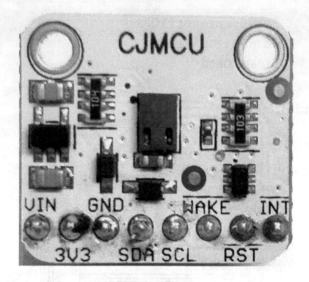

In our circuit, we are utilizing this sensor for detecting TVOC as well as CO2 accessible in nature and showing the information on 16*2 LCD.

Pin Configuration

Pin No.	Pin Name	Description
1	Vin	Input Supply (3.3v to 5v)
2	3V3	3.3V output Pin for external use
3	Gnd	Ground
4	SDA	This is I2C clock pin
5	SCL	I2C data pin
6	WAKE	Wakeup Pin of sensor, should

		be connected to ground in order to communicate with the sensor
7	RST	Reset pin: When connected to ground the sensor reset itself
8	INT	This is interrupt output pin, used to detect when a new reading is ready or when a reading gets too high or low

Application

- Cell phones

- Wearables

- Home and Building Automation

- Embellishments

Code and Explanation

The total Arduino code for TVOC as well as CO2 Measurement utilizing CCS811 Air Quality Sensor is given toward the end.

In the beneath code, we are characterizing the libraries for 16*2 LCD as well as CCS811 Air Quality Sensor. For downloading the library "Adafruit_CCS811.h" for

CCS811 pursue this connection.

```
#include <LiquidCrystal.h>

#include "Adafruit_CCS811.h"
```

Beneath we have characterized Pins for association of 16*2 LCD with Arduino.

```
LiquidCrystal lcd(12, 13, 8, 9, 10, 11); /// REGIS-TER SELECT PIN,ENABLE PIN,D4 PIN,D5 PIN, D6 PIN, D7 PIN

Adafruit_CCS811 ccs;
```

Beneath we have set up LCD and CCS811 air quality sensor and adjusted it for the indicating right temperature, as appeared in the underneath code,

```
void setup() {

  lcd.begin(16, 2);

  ccs.begin();

  //calibrate temperature sensor
```

```
while(!ccs.available());

float temp = ccs.calculateTemperature();

ccs.setTempOffset(temp - 25.0);

}
```

In the beneath code, we utilized capacities "ccs.available()" (Function is as of now characterized in library) to check if there is a few information coming. As we get the information we can figure the temperature and show it on 16*2 LCD.

Further in the event that CCS is accessible and ccs.readData() is returning false then we get the CO2 worth utilizing capacity ccs.geteCO2() as well as TVOC worth utilizing ccs.getTVOC(), as appeared in the beneath code. Consequently, we have gotten the estimation of air quality parameters utilizing CCS811 air quality sensor.

```
void loop() {

  if(ccs.available()){

    float temp = ccs.calculateTemperature();

    if(!ccs.readData()){
```

```
    int co2 = ccs.geteCO2();

    int tvoc = ccs.getTVOC();

    lcd.setCursor(0, 0);

    lcd.print(String ("CO2:")+ String (co2)+String("
PPM"));

    lcd.setCursor(0, 1);

    lcd.print(String  ("TVOC:")+  String  (tvoc)
+String(" PPB "));

    lcd.print(String("T:"+String       (int(temp)))
+String("C"));

    delay(3000);

    lcd.clear();

  }

  else{

  lcd.print("ERROR");

  while(1);

  }
```

```
  }

}
```

Complete Arduino code is given beneath. Code is straightforward, all the work is finished by its library itself and we have utilized capacities characterized in the CCS library to get the estimations of CO2 as well as TOVC.

Likewise, check:

- IOT based Air Pollution Monitoring System utilizing Arduino

- Estimating PPM from MQ Gas Sensors utilizing Arduino

Code

```
#include <LiquidCrystal.h>
#include "Adafruit_CCS811.h"

LiquidCrystal lcd(12, 13, 8, 9, 10, 11); /// REGISTER
SELECT PIN,ENABLE PIN,D4 PIN,D5 PIN, D6 PIN, D7
PIN
Adafruit_CCS811 ccs;

void setup() {
 lcd.begin(16, 2);
 ccs.begin();
 //calibrate temperature sensor
 while(!ccs.available());
```

```
 float temp = ccs.calculateTemperature();
 ccs.setTempOffset(temp - 25.0);
}
void loop() {
 if(ccs.available()){
  float temp = ccs.calculateTemperature();
  if(!ccs.readData()){
   int co2 = ccs.geteCO2();
   int tvoc = ccs.getTVOC();
   lcd.setCursor(0, 0);
      lcd.print(String ("CO2:")+ String (co2)+String("
PPM"));


    lcd.setCursor(0, 1);
    lcd.print(String ("TVOC:")+ String (tvoc)+String("
PPB "));
              lcd.print(String("T:"+String   (int(temp)))
+String("C"));
   delay(3000);
   lcd.clear();
  }
  else{
  lcd.print("ERROR");
  while(1);
  }
 }
}
```

2.ARDUINO BASED COUNTDOWN TIMER

A clock is a kind of clock utilized for the estimation of time interims. There are two kinds of clock, one which checks upwards from zero, for the estimation of the slipped by time, called as Stopwatch. What's more, the subsequent one checks down from a predefined time span given by the client, for the most part called as Countdown Timer.

Here, in this instructional exercise we will tell you the best way to make a Countdown Timer utilizing Arduino. Here we are not utilizing any Real Time Clock (RTC) module for getting the time. The time span is furnished by the client with the assistance of Keypad and 16x2 LCD. Also, when the clock compasses to Zero, ready sound will be created with the assistance of Buzzer.

Material Required

- LCD 16*2
- Arduino UNO
- Buzzer
- 4*4 matrix keypad
- Potentiometer (10k)
- Pushbutton
- Connecting wires
- Resistor (10k, 100 ohm)

Circuit Diagram

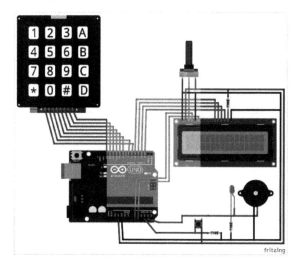

Arduino Uno is utilized here as primary controller. A keypad is utilized for nourishing the time length and a 16*2 LCD is utilized to show the commencement. The pushbutton is utilized to begin the time. Check here how to interface 4x4 Keypad with Arduino and 16x2 LCD with Arduino.

Code and Explanation

Complete Arduino Timer code is given toward the part of the arrangement.

In this code beneath, we are introducing libraries for keypad and LCD and the factors utilized in the code.

```
#include <LiquidCrystal.h>

#include <Keypad.h>

long int set1;

long int set2;

long int set3;

long int set4;

long int j;

int t1, t2, t3, t4, t5, t6;

int r1, r2, r3;

char key;

String r[8];
```

```
String hours;

String minutes;

String seconds;
```

Presently, in the beneath code we are introducing the no. of lines and sections for characterizing the lattice for keypad.

```
const byte ROWS = 4; // Four rows

const byte COLS = 4; // Three columns

char keys[ROWS][COLS] = {

  {'1','2','3','A'},

  {'4','5','6','B'},

  {'7','8','9','C'},

  {'*','0','#','D'}

};
```

For associating the 4*4 network keypad with Arduino we need to characterize the pins for the lines and sections. So in beneath code we have characterized pins for Keypad just as 16x2 LCD.

```
byte rowPins[ROWS] = { 6, 7, 8, 9 };// Connect key-
pad ROW0, ROW1, ROW2 and ROW3 to these Ar-
duino pins

byte colPins[COLS] = { 10, 11, 12, 13 };// Connect
keypad COL0, COL1 and COL2 to t

LiquidCrystal lcd(A0, A1, 5, 4, 3, 2); // Creates an
LC object. Parameters: (rs, enable, d4, d5, d6, d7)
```

The underneath code is utilized for making the key-pad,

```
Keypad kpd = Keypad( makeKeymap(keys), row-
Pins, colPins, ROWS, COLS );
```

In the void setFeedingTime() work code, in the wake of squeezing the pushbutton we can enter the ideal opportunity for clock, at that point subsequent to entering the clock time span, we need to Press D to start the commencement.

```
void setFeedingTime()

{
```

```
feed = true;

 int i=0;

lcd.clear();

lcd.setCursor(0,0);

lcd.print("Set feeding Time");

lcd.clear();

lcd.print("HH:MM:SS");

lcd.setCursor(0,1);

while(1){

  key = kpd.getKey();

  char j;

if(key!=NO_KEY){

  lcd.setCursor(j,1);

  lcd.print(key);

  r[i] = key-48;
```

```
   i++;

   j++;

   if (j==2 || j == 5)

   {

    lcd.print(":"); j++;

   }

   delay(500);

 }

 if (key == 'D')

 {key=0; break; }

 }

 lcd.clear();

}
```

In void arrangement() work, we have introduced the LCD and sequential correspondence, and characterized the pins as INPUT as well as OUTPUT in the beneath code.

```
void setup()

{

  lcd.begin(16,2);

  Serial.begin(9600);

  pinMode(A0, OUTPUT);

  pinMode(A1, OUTPUT);

  pinMode(A3, INPUT);

  pinMode(A4, OUTPUT);

}
```

Working of this Arduino Timer is straightforward however the code is somewhat mind boggling. The code is clarified by the remarks in the code.

At first, it will print "Arduino Timer" on the LCD show until you press the pushbutton. When you press the pushbutton, it will request to enter commencement time span by calling the "setFeedingTime" work. At that point you can enter the time span with the assistance of Keypad. At that point you have to squeeze

'D' to spare the time and start the commencement clock. Here in void circle() work, we have done some estimation to decrement the time step by step and to demonstrate the best possible estimations of Hour, Minutes and Seconds (HH:MM:SS) as indicated by the rest of the time. All the code is all around clarified by remarks. You can check the total code underneath.

As the clock ranges to zero, the bell starts signaling and blares for multiple times just (according to the code). To stop the bell, press and hold the pushbutton. You can use the Pushbutton whenever to stop the clock in the middle of tallying.

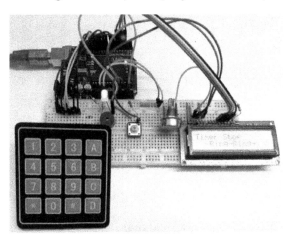

Code

```
#include <LiquidCrystal.h>
#include <Keypad.h>
const byte ROWS = 4; // Four rows
const byte COLS = 4; // Three columns
long int set1;
long int set2;
long int set3;
long int set4;
long int j;
String hours;
String minutes;
String seconds;
// Define the Keymap
char keys[ROWS][COLS] = {
  {'1','2','3','A'},
  {'4','5','6','B'},
```

```
  {'7','8','9','C'},
  {'*','0','#','D'}
};
byte rowPins[ROWS] = { 6, 7, 8, 9 };// Connect key-
pad ROW0, ROW1, ROW2 and ROW3 to these Arduino
pins
byte colPins[COLS] = { 10, 11, 12, 13 };// Connect key-
pad COL0, COL1 and COL2 to t
Keypad kpd = Keypad( makeKeymap(keys), rowPins,
colPins, ROWS, COLS );
LiquidCrystal lcd(A0, A1, 5, 4, 3, 2); // Creates an LC
object. Parameters: (rs, enable, d4, d5, d6, d7)
int t1, t2, t3, t4, t5, t6;
int r1, r2, r3;


boolean feed = true; // condition for alarm
char key;
String r[8];
void setFeedingTime()
{
  feed = true;
  int i=0;
  lcd.clear();
  lcd.setCursor(0,0);
  lcd.print("Set feeding Time");
  lcd.clear();
  lcd.print("HH:MM:SS");
  lcd.setCursor(0,1);
```

```
while(1){
key = kpd.getKey();
char j;


if(key!=NO_KEY){


  lcd.setCursor(j,1);


  lcd.print(key);


  r[i] = key-48;
i++;
j++;
if(j==2 || j == 5)
{
 lcd.print(":");j++;
}
 delay(500);
}
if(key == 'D')
{key=0; break;}
}
lcd.clear();
}
```

```
void setup()
{
lcd.begin(16,2);
Serial.begin(9600);
pinMode(A0, OUTPUT);
pinMode(A1, OUTPUT);
pinMode(A3, INPUT);
pinMode(A4, OUTPUT);
}


void loop()
{
  lcd.setCursor(0,0);
  lcd.print("Arduino Timer");
  //Serial.println(A3);
  if(digitalRead(A3)==1) //
  {
  lcd.clear();
  setFeedingTime();
  for(int i = 0; i < 6; i++) // this for loop is used to get
the value of the feeding time and print it serially
  {
   Serial.print(r[i]);
   Serial.println();
  }


  hours = String(r[0]) + String(r[1]) ; //combining two
separate int values of r[0] and r[1] into one string and
```

save it to "hours"

   minutes = String (r[2]) + String (r[3]) ; //combining two separate int values of r[2] and r[3] into one string and save it to "minutes"

   seconds = String (r[4]) + String (r[5]) ; //combining two separate int values of r[4] and r[5] into one string and save it to "seconds"

 set1 = (hours.toInt()*3600); //converting hours into seconds

 set2 = (minutes.toInt() * 60); //converting minutes into seconds

 set3 = seconds.toInt();

 set4 = (hours.toInt() * 3600)+ (minutes.toInt() * 60) + seconds.toInt(); //adding set1, set2 and set3 together in set4

 Serial.print("set4");

 Serial.print(set4);

 Serial.println();

 lcd.setCursor(0,0);

 lcd.print("Countdown begins");

 delay(1000);

 lcd.clear();

  for(long int j = set4; j >= 0; j--) // this for loop is used to decrease the total time in seconds

 {

 Serial.println(j);

```
 lcd.setCursor(0,0);
 lcd.print("HH:MM:SS");


 long int HH = j / 3600; // converting the remaining
time into remaining hours
 lcd.setCursor(0,1);
 Serial.println(HH);
 if(HH < 10){lcd.print('0'); }
 lcd.print(HH);
 lcd.print(":");


 long int MM = (j - (HH*3600))/60 ; //converting the
remaining time into remaining minutes
 lcd.setCursor(3,1);
 Serial.println(MM);
 if(MM < 10){lcd.print('0'); }
 lcd.print(MM);
 lcd.print(":");


 long int SS = j - ((HH*3600)+(MM*60)); //converting
the remaining time into remaining seconds
 lcd.setCursor(6,1);
 Serial.println(SS);
 if(SS < 10){lcd.print('0'); }
 lcd.print(SS);
 delay(1000);
 if(digitalRead(A3)==1){break;}
```

```
if (j == 0)

   {
   lcd.clear();
   lcd.setCursor(0,0);
   lcd.print("Timer Stop");
   lcd.setCursor(2,1);
   lcd.print("-Ring-Ring-");


   for(int k =0; k<= 100; k++) //this for loop is used
for the buzzer to beep 100 time as the timer reaches
zero
   {
   digitalWrite(A4,HIGH);
   delay(300);
   digitalWrite(A4,LOW);
   delay(300);
   if(digitalRead(A3)==1){break;}
   }
  }
 }
 }
}
```

3.INTERFACING GRAPHICAL LCD (ST7920) WITH ARDUINO

There are bunches of LCDs utilized in Electronic Projects. We have just utilized 16X2 LCD in a significant number of our activities and furthermore utilized TFT LCD with Arduino. You can locate our whole 16X2 LCD related venture by following this connection, incorporating interfacing with 8051, AVR, Arduino and some more.

The ST9720 Graphical LCD is entirely unexpected from the Ordinary LCDs. Standard LCD can just print straightforward content or numbers inside a fixed size. In any case, in Graphical LCDs we have 128*64 which is equivalent to 8192 spots or 8192/8 = 1024 pixels, so separated from character, we can show any Graphical Image in this GLCD.

We as of now interfaced GLCD with 8051, today we will interface Graphical LCD with Arduino to show content and pictures on it.

Material Required

- Arduino UNO
- 128*64 Graphical LCD ST9720
- Potentiometer-10k
- Connecting wires
- Breadboard

Circuit Diagram

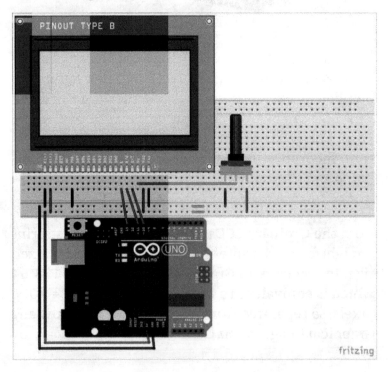

128*64 Graphical LCD

This Graphical LCD is having low power utilization and furthermore reasonable for battery control versatile gadget. It have wide working voltage go 2.2v to 5.5v and bolsters both sequential and 8/4-piece parallel correspondence and accompanies ST7290 LCD controller/driver IC. Interface correspondence mode can be exchanged among parallel and sequential utilizing PSB PIN 15. This graphical LCD has a programmed power on Reset work and can be effectively constrained by MCU, for example, 8051, AVR, ARM, Arduino and Raspberry Pi.

You can proceed with the datasheet for definite data about ST 7290 128*64 Graphical LCD

Pin Configuration

Pin No.	Pin Name	Description
1	Gnd	Ground terminal
2	Vcc	Input supply voltage (2.7v to 5.5v)
3	Vo	LCD contrast
4	RS	Register Select RS = 0: Instruction Register RS = 1: Data Register
5	R/W	Read/Write control

6	E	Enable
7,8,9,10,11,12,13,14	DB0, DB1, DB2, DB3, DB4, DB5, DB6, DB7	Data Pins (used in parallel 8/4bit communication mode)
15	PSB	Interface selection: Low(0) for serial communication mode High (1) for 8/4-bit parallel bus mode.
16	NC	Not connected
17	RST	Reset Pin
18	Vout	LCD voltage doubler output. VOUT $\leqq$ 7V.
19	BLA	Backlight positive supply
20	BLK	Backlight Negative supply

Applications

- Mechanical gadget

- Inserted Systems

- Security

- Restorative

- Hand-held gear

Converting Image into Hex Code:

To demonstrate any picture on Graphical LCD, we need HEX code of that picture, so here are not many strides to change over Image into HEX code. Before that you need to ensure that the size of picture ought not surpass 128*64.

Step-1: Minimize the size of the ordinary picture to 128*64 or less, which you can do utilizing any picture altering programming like MS paint.

As appeared in the image above, we are setting the width and stature of the picture to 128*64.

Step-2: Then you have to spare the picture in "image_ name.bmp" design.

Select the arrangement appeared in the above picture and spare the record for further procedure.

Step-3: After sparing it into ".bmp" design you have to change over the picture into hex code for printing. For this, I am utilizing the product named GIMP 2, which convert Bmp record to hex code.

As appeared in the picture above, we opened the ".bmp" design document in the GIMP 2 programming.

Step-4: After downloading the product, open the BMP organization picture record which you need to print and afterward spare as it in ".xbm" (X BitMap)format. Subsequent to sparing it open that record utilizing Notepad and you will get the Hex code of the picture.

As appeared in the image underneath, pick the Export choice to spare the record in the xbm group:

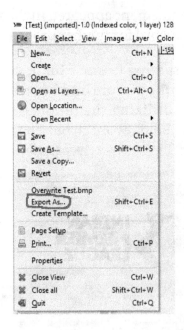

Select the arrangement appeared in the image beneath and send out the picture document.

Subsequent to sending out the record, you will get the document in ".xbm" design. Open the xbm record utilizing Notepad and you will get the HEX code as appeared in picture underneath.

```
Test.xbm - Notepad
File  Edit  Format  View  Help
#define 123_width 128
#define 123_height 64
static unsigned char 123_bits[] = {
 0x00, 0x00, 0x00, 0x00, 0x00, 0x00, 0x00, 0x00, 0x00, 0x00, 0x00, 0x00,
 0x00, 0x00, 0x00, 0x00, 0x00, 0x00, 0x00, 0x00, 0x00, 0x00, 0x00, 0x00,
 0x00, 0x00, 0x00, 0x00, 0x00, 0x00, 0x00, 0x00, 0x00, 0x00, 0x00, 0x00,
 0x00, 0x00, 0x00, 0x00, 0x00, 0x00, 0x00, 0x00, 0x00, 0x00, 0x00, 0x00,
 0x00, 0x00, 0x00, 0x00, 0x00, 0x00, 0x00, 0x00, 0x00, 0x00, 0x00, 0x00,
 0x00, 0x00, 0x00, 0x00, 0x00, 0x00, 0x00, 0x00, 0x00, 0x00, 0x00, 0x00,
 0x00, 0x00, 0x00, 0x00, 0x00, 0x00, 0x00, 0x00, 0x00, 0x00, 0x00, 0x00,
 0x00, 0x00, 0x00, 0x00, 0x00, 0x00, 0x00, 0x00, 0x00, 0x00, 0x00, 0x00,
 0x00, 0x00, 0x00, 0x00, 0x00, 0x00, 0x00, 0x00, 0x00, 0x00, 0x00, 0x00,
 0x00, 0x00, 0x00, 0x00, 0x00, 0x00, 0x00, 0x00, 0x00, 0x00, 0x00, 0x00,
 0x00, 0x00, 0x00, 0x00, 0x00, 0x00, 0x00, 0x00, 0x00, 0x00, 0x00, 0x00,
 0x00, 0x00, 0x00, 0x00, 0x00, 0x00, 0x00, 0x00, 0x00, 0x00, 0x00, 0x00,
 0x00, 0x00, 0xfc, 0x01, 0x00, 0x00, 0x00, 0x00, 0x00, 0x00, 0x00, 0x00,
 0x00, 0x00, 0x00, 0x00, 0x00, 0x80, 0x63, 0x03, 0x00, 0x00, 0x00, 0x00,
 0x00, 0x00, 0x00, 0x00, 0x00, 0x00, 0x00, 0x00, 0x00, 0xfe, 0xff, 0x03,
 0x00, 0x00, 0x00, 0x00, 0x00, 0x00, 0x00, 0x00, 0x00, 0x00, 0x00, 0x00,
 0x86, 0xff, 0xff, 0x03, 0x00, 0x78, 0x0e, 0xee, 0x3f, 0x7c, 0x70, 0xf0,
 0xe0, 0x00, 0x00, 0x00, 0x00, 0xfe, 0xff, 0xfc, 0x02, 0x00, 0x78, 0x1e, 0xee,
 0xff, 0x7c, 0xf8, 0xf0, 0xe1, 0x00, 0x00, 0x00, 0xfe, 0x07, 0xf0, 0x01,
 0x00, 0x78, 0x3e, 0xee, 0xff, 0x7d, 0xf8, 0xf0, 0xe3, 0x00, 0x00, 0x00,
 0x00, 0xf8, 0xf0, 0x01, 0x00, 0x78, 0x7e, 0xce, 0xf3, 0x7f, 0xf8, 0xf0,
 0xe7, 0x00, 0x00, 0x00, 0x00, 0xfc, 0xf0, 0x01, 0x00, 0x78, 0xfe, 0xce,
 0xe3, 0x7f, 0xfc, 0xf1, 0x67, 0x00, 0x00, 0x00, 0x00, 0xfc, 0xf3, 0x00,
 0x00, 0x78, 0xfe, 0xcf, 0xe3, 0x7b, 0xfc, 0xf1, 0x6f, 0x00, 0x00, 0x00,
```

← Hex code

Arduino Code and Working Explanation

To interface graphical LCD with Arduino, first we have to characterize the library utilized for the Graphical LCD. Arduino don't have this library, you have to install and introduce this library from this connection. At that point you can incorporate the library like beneath:

#include "U8glib.h"

Here, 'u8g(10)' is characterizing the association of RS(Register Select) stick of graphical LCD with the tenth stick of the Arduino UNO. RS stick utilized as 'chip select' and 'Register Select' when utilized in Serial and Parallel mode separately. Along these lines, we are utilizing the sequential mode and RS stick set to High (1) for chip empowered and Low (0) for chip crippled.

```
U8GLIB_ST7920_128X64_4X u8g(10);
```

Presently, for printing the picture we have to put the Hex code of the picture in the underneath code. You can print some other picture you just should simply glue the hex code of the picture.

```
const uint8_t rook_bitmap[] U8G_PROGMEM = {

Paste the Hex code of image here

};
```

Check the Full Arduino Code toward the finish of this Article.

The beneath capacity is utilized for printing picture, the direction utilized for printing is "u8g.drawXBM-P(x, y, width of picture, tallness of picture)". Where, X and Y is the beginning situation of the picture on LCD and we additionally need to compose the size of the picture which ought not surpass 128*64 and in definite contention we have called work in which we put the HEX code of picture.

```
void picture(void) {
```

```
u8g.drawXBMP( 0, 0, 128, 64, rook_bitmap);

}
```

We have made two capacities called "draw" and "next", in which the code for printing the substance is composed utilizing order "u8g.drawStr(x,y,"abcd")". Here, x and y are the situation in the LCD where the substance will be printed and 'abcd' is the substance to be print.

```
void draw(void) {

  u8g.setFont(u8g_font_unifont);

   u8g.drawStr( 07, 35, "Hello World");

}

void next(void) {

  u8g.setFont(u8g_font_unifont);

  u8g.drawStr( 0, 15, "Interfacing");

  u8g.drawStr( 0, 35, "Graphical LCD");

  u8g.drawStr( 0, 55, "with Arduino");
```

```
}
```

clearLCD() work is made for clearing the LCD by simply giving invalid an incentive to the capacity.

```
void clearLCD(){

  u8g.firstPage();

  do {

  } while( u8g.nextPage() );

}
```

Setting up pixel, shading and force by utilizing the code beneath

```
void setup(void) {

  if ( u8g.getMode() == U8G_MODE_R3G3B2 ) {

    u8g.setColorIndex(255);   // white

  }

  else  if  (  u8g.getMode()  ==  U8G_MODE_G-
```

```
RAY2BIT ){

  u8g.setColorIndex(3);    // max intensity

}

else if ( u8g.getMode() == U8G_MODE_BW ){

  u8g.setColorIndex(1);    // pixel on

}

else if ( u8g.getMode() == U8G_MODE_HIC-
OLOR ){

  u8g.setHiColorByRGB(255,255,255);

}

}
```

The void circle keeps on printing the content and picture after the given postponement. Initially, we have printed "Hello world" utilizing draw work and after 2sec. of defer we cleared the screen utilizing clearLCD capacity and after that print "Interfacing Graphical LCD utilizing Arduino" utilizing next capacity. At that point we have printed the picture utilizing picture() work which will remain on screen for 3 seconds. This will proceed till the power supply is turned on.

```
void loop(void) {

  u8g.firstPage();

  do {

    draw();

  } while( u8g.nextPage() );

  delay(2000);

  clearLCD();

  u8g.firstPage();

  do {

    next();

  } while( u8g.nextPage() );

    delay(2000);

  clearLCD();

  u8g.firstPage();
```

```
do {

  picture();

} while( u8g.nextPage() );

 delay(3000);

 clearLCD();

 delay(50);

}
```

Subsequent to programming the Arduino utilizing the given code, interface the Graphical LCD according to the circuit outline with the Arduino as well as supply the Arduino utilizing Adapter or USB. You, will get substance and picture imprinted on the Graphical LCD,
Likewise check interfacing Nokia 5110 Graphical LCD with Arduino,

Code

```
#include "U8glib.h"
U8GLIB_ST7920_128X64_4X u8g(10);
const uint8_t rook_bitmap[] U8G_PROGMEM = {
0x00, 0x00, 0x00, 0x00, 0x00, 0x00, 0x00, 0x00,
0x00, 0x00, 0x00, 0x00,
  0x00, 0x00, 0x00, 0x00, 0x00, 0x00, 0x00, 0x00,
```

```
0x00, 0x00, 0x00, 0x00,
  0x00, 0x00, 0x00, 0x00, 0x00, 0x00, 0x00, 0x00,
0x00, 0x00, 0x00, 0x00,
  0x00, 0x00, 0x00, 0x00, 0x00, 0x00, 0x00, 0x00,
0x00, 0x00, 0x00, 0x00,
  0x00, 0x00, 0x00, 0x00, 0x00, 0x00, 0x00, 0x00,
0x00, 0x00, 0x00, 0x00,
  0x00, 0x00, 0x00, 0x00, 0x00, 0x00, 0x00, 0x00,
0x00, 0x00, 0x00, 0x00,
  0x00, 0x00, 0x00, 0x00, 0x00, 0x00, 0x00, 0x00,
0x00, 0x00, 0x00, 0x00,
  0x00, 0x00, 0x00, 0x00, 0x00, 0x00, 0x00, 0x00,
0x00, 0x00, 0x00, 0x00,
  0x00, 0x00, 0x00, 0x00, 0x00, 0x00, 0x00, 0x00,
0x00, 0x00, 0x00, 0x00,
  0x00, 0x00, 0x00, 0x00, 0x00, 0x00, 0x00, 0x00,
0x00, 0x00, 0x00, 0x00,
  0x00, 0x00, 0x00, 0x00, 0x00, 0x00, 0x00, 0x00,
0x00, 0x00, 0x00, 0x00,
  0x00, 0x00, 0x00, 0x00, 0x00, 0x00, 0x00, 0x00,
0x00, 0x00, 0x00, 0x00,
  0x00, 0x00, 0xfc, 0x01, 0x00, 0x00, 0x00, 0x00,
0x00, 0x00, 0x00, 0x00,
  0x00, 0x00, 0x00, 0x00, 0x00, 0x80, 0x63, 0x03,
0x00, 0x00, 0x00, 0x00,
  0x00, 0x00, 0x00, 0x00, 0x00, 0x00, 0x00, 0x00,
0x00, 0xfe, 0xff, 0x03,
  0x00, 0x00, 0x00, 0x00, 0x00, 0x00, 0x00, 0x00,
0x00, 0x00, 0x00, 0x00,
  0x86, 0xff, 0xff, 0x03, 0x00, 0x78, 0x0e, 0xee, 0x3f,
```

0x7c,0x70,0xf0,

0xe0,0x00,0x00,0x00,0xfe,0xff,0xfc,0x02,0x00,
0x78,0x1e,0xee,

0xff,0x7c,0xf8,0xf0,0xe1,0x00,0x00,0x00,0xfe,
0x07,0xf0,0x01,

0x00,0x78,0x3e,0xee,0xff,0x7d,0xf8,0xf0,0xe3,
0x00,0x00,0x00,

0x00, 0xf8, 0xf0, 0x01, 0x00, 0x78, 0x7e, 0xce,
0xf3,0x7f,0xf8,0xf0,

0xe7, 0x00, 0x00, 0x00, 0x00, 0xfc, 0xf0, 0x01,
0x00,0x78,0xfe,0xce,

0xe3, 0x7f, 0xfc, 0xf1, 0x67, 0x00, 0x00, 0x00,
0x00,0xfc,0xf3,0x00,

0x00,0x78,0xfe,0xcf,0xe3,0x7b,0xfc,0xf1,0x6f,
0x00,0x00,0x00,

0x00,0xfc,0xfb,0x00,0x00,0x78,0xfe,0xcf,0xc3,
0x7b,0xee,0xf3,

0x7f,0x00,0x00,0x00,0x00,0xfc,0xff,0x00,0x00,
0x78,0xf6,0xcf,

0xe3, 0x7b, 0xfe, 0x73, 0x7f, 0x00, 0x00, 0x00,
0x00,0xfc,0x7f,0x00,

0x00,0x78,0xe6,0xcf,0xe3,0x7f,0xff,0x77,0x7e,
0x00,0x00,0x00,

0x00,0xf8,0x7f,0x00,0x00,0x78,0xc6,0xcf,0xe3,
0x7d,0xff,0x77,

0x7c, 0x00, 0x00, 0x00, 0x00, 0xf8, 0x3f, 0x00,
0x00,0x78,0x86,0xcf,

0xfb, 0xfd, 0xc7, 0x7f, 0x78, 0x00, 0x00, 0x00,
0x00,0xf8,0x3f,0x00,

0x00,0x78,0x0e,0xef,0xff,0xfc,0x83,0x7f,0x70,

0x00, 0x00, 0x00,
  0x00, 0xf0, 0x7f, 0x00, 0x00, 0x78, 0x0e, 0xee,
0x3f, 0xfc, 0x83, 0x7f,
  0xf0, 0x00, 0x00, 0x00, 0x00, 0xf0, 0xff, 0x00,
0x00, 0x00, 0x00, 0x00,
  0x00, 0x00, 0x00, 0x00, 0x00, 0x00, 0x00, 0x00,
0x00, 0xf0, 0xff, 0x01,
  0x00, 0x00, 0x00, 0x00, 0x00, 0x00, 0x00, 0x00,
0x00, 0x00, 0x00, 0x00,
  0x00, 0xf0, 0xff, 0x01, 0x00, 0xf8, 0xe7, 0x1f, 0xfe,
0x79, 0xe0, 0x7c,
  0xff, 0xfe, 0x01, 0x00, 0x00, 0xc0, 0xff, 0x03, 0x00,
0xf8, 0xef, 0x7f,
  0xfe, 0x79, 0xf0, 0x7c, 0xff, 0xfe, 0x07, 0x00, 0x00,
0x80, 0xff, 0x07,
  0x00, 0xf8, 0xef, 0x7f, 0xfe, 0x79, 0xf0, 0x7c, 0xff,
0xfe, 0x07, 0x00,
  0x00, 0x00, 0xff, 0x07, 0x00, 0x78, 0xef, 0x7b,
0x1e, 0xf8, 0xf8, 0x7c,
  0x0f, 0xbe, 0x07, 0x00, 0x00, 0x00, 0xfe, 0x0f,
0x00, 0x78, 0xef, 0x7b,
  0x1e, 0xfc, 0xf8, 0x7d, 0x0f, 0xbe, 0x07, 0x00,
0x00, 0x00, 0xfc, 0x3f,
  0x00, 0x78, 0xcf, 0x7b, 0xfe, 0xfc, 0xfd, 0x7d, 0xff,
0xfe, 0x07, 0x00,
  0x00, 0x00, 0xf8, 0x3f, 0x00, 0xf8, 0xcf, 0x7f, 0xfe,
0xfc, 0xfd, 0x7d,
  0xff, 0xfe, 0x07, 0x00, 0x00, 0x00, 0xf0, 0x7f, 0x00,
0xf8, 0xc3, 0x1f,
  0xfe, 0xfc, 0xff, 0x7d, 0xff, 0xfe, 0x01, 0x00, 0x00,

0x00, 0xf0, 0xff,
0x00, 0x78, 0xe0, 0x3f, 0x1e, 0xfc, 0xef, 0x7d, 0x0f,
0xfe, 0x03, 0x00,
0x00, 0x00, 0xf0, 0xff, 0x01, 0x78, 0xe0, 0x7f, 0x1e,
0xdc, 0xef, 0x7d,
0x0f, 0xfe, 0x07, 0x00, 0x00, 0x00, 0xf0, 0xff, 0x03,
0x78, 0xe0, 0x7f,
0xfe, 0xdd, 0xe7, 0x7d, 0xff, 0xff, 0x07, 0x00, 0x00,
0x00, 0xe0, 0xff,
0x03, 0x78, 0xe0, 0xfb, 0xfe, 0x9d, 0xe7, 0x7d, 0xff,
0xbf, 0x0f, 0x00,
0x00, 0x00, 0xe0, 0xff, 0x07, 0x78, 0xe0, 0xfb, 0xfe,
0x9f, 0xe3, 0x7f,
0xff, 0xbf, 0x0f, 0x00, 0x00, 0x00, 0xe0, 0xff, 0x07,
0x00, 0x00, 0x00,
0x00, 0x00, 0x00, 0x00, 0x00, 0x00, 0x00, 0x00,
0x00, 0x00, 0xc0, 0xff,
0x0f, 0x00, 0x00, 0x00, 0x00, 0x00, 0x00, 0x00,
0x00, 0x00, 0x00, 0x00,
0x00, 0x00, 0xc0, 0xff, 0x3f, 0x78, 0xf0, 0x0f, 0x1c,
0xe0, 0xcf, 0xc3,
0xfd, 0x03, 0x00, 0x00, 0x00, 0x00, 0xc0, 0xff, 0x3f,
0x78, 0xf0, 0x0f,
0x1e, 0xf8, 0xcf, 0xc3, 0xfd, 0x03, 0x00, 0x00, 0x00,
0x00, 0xc0, 0xff,
0x3f, 0x78, 0xf0, 0x0f, 0x3e, 0xfc, 0xce, 0xc3, 0xfd,
0x03, 0x00, 0x00,
0x00, 0x00, 0xc0, 0xff, 0x1f, 0x78, 0xf0, 0x00, 0x3f,
0x3c, 0xcc, 0xc3,
0x79, 0x00, 0x00, 0x00, 0x00, 0x00, 0xc0, 0xff,

0x0f, 0x78, 0xf0, 0x00,
  0x7f, 0x3e, 0xc0, 0xc3, 0x79, 0x00, 0x00, 0x00,
0x00, 0x00, 0xe0, 0xff,
  0x03, 0x78, 0xf0, 0x8f, 0x7f, 0x1e, 0xc0, 0xc3, 0xf9,
0x03, 0x00, 0x00,
  0x00, 0x00, 0xf0, 0xff, 0x01, 0x78, 0xf0, 0x8f, 0x7b,
0x1e, 0xc0, 0xc3,
  0xf9, 0x03, 0x00, 0x00, 0x00, 0x00, 0xf8, 0xff,
0x00, 0x78, 0xf0, 0x8f,
  0xff, 0x1e, 0xdf, 0xc3, 0xf9, 0x03, 0x00, 0x00, 0x00,
0x00, 0xfc, 0x7f,
  0x00, 0x78, 0xf0, 0xc0, 0xff, 0x3e, 0xde, 0xc3, 0x79,
0x00, 0x00, 0x00,
  0x00, 0x00, 0xfc, 0x3f, 0x00, 0x78, 0xf0, 0xc0, 0xff,
0x3f, 0xde, 0xc3,
  0x79, 0x00, 0x00, 0x00, 0x00, 0x00, 0xfe, 0x1f,
0x00, 0xf8, 0xfe, 0xfd,
  0xf1, 0x7d, 0xde, 0xe7, 0x7d, 0x07, 0x00, 0x00,
0x00, 0x00, 0xfe, 0x0f,
  0x00, 0xf8, 0xff, 0xff, 0xf0, 0xff, 0x9f, 0xff, 0xfc,
0x07, 0x00, 0x00,
  0x00, 0x00, 0xff, 0x07, 0x00, 0xf8, 0xff, 0xff, 0xe0,
0xf3, 0x1f, 0x7f,
  0xfc, 0x07, 0x00, 0x00, 0x00, 0x80, 0xff, 0x01,
0x00, 0x00, 0x00, 0x00,
  0x00, 0x00, 0x00, 0x00, 0x00, 0x00, 0x00, 0x00,
0x00, 0xc0, 0xff, 0x01,
  0x00, 0x00, 0x00, 0x00, 0x00, 0x00, 0x00, 0x00,
0x00, 0x00, 0x00, 0x00,
  0x00, 0xc0, 0x9f, 0x01, 0x00, 0x00, 0x00, 0x00,

```
0x00, 0x00, 0x00, 0x00,
  0x00, 0x00, 0x00, 0x00, 0x00, 0xc0, 0x0e, 0x00,
0x00, 0x00, 0x00, 0x00,
  0x00, 0x00, 0x00, 0x00, 0x00, 0x00, 0x00, 0x00,
0x00, 0xc0, 0x07, 0x00,
  0x00, 0x00, 0x00, 0x00, 0x00, 0x00, 0x00, 0x00,
0x00, 0x00, 0x00, 0x00,
  0x00, 0xc0, 0x07, 0x00, 0x00, 0x00, 0x00, 0x00,
0x00, 0x00, 0x00, 0x00,
  0x00, 0x00, 0x00, 0x00, 0x00, 0x00, 0x00, 0x00,
0x00, 0x00, 0x00, 0x00,
  0x00, 0x00, 0x00, 0x00, 0x00, 0x00, 0x00, 0x00,
0x00, 0x00, 0x00, 0x00,
  0x00, 0x00, 0x00, 0x00, 0x00, 0x00, 0x00, 0x00,
0x00, 0x00, 0x00, 0x00,
  0x00, 0x00, 0x00, 0x00, 0x00, 0x00, 0x00, 0x00,
0x00, 0x00, 0x00, 0x00,
 0x00, 0x00, 0x00, 0x00
 };
void draw(void) {
 //u8g.setFont(u8g_font_unifont);
 u8g.setFont(u8g_font_osb18);
 u8g.drawStr( 07, 27, "HELLO");
 u8g.drawStr( 12, 52, "WORLD");
}
void picture(void) {
 u8g.drawXBMP( 0, 0, 128, 64, rook_bitmap);
}
void next(void) {
 u8g.setFont(u8g_font_unifont);
```

```
//u8g.setFont(u8g_font_osb18);
u8g.drawStr( 07, 18, "Interfacing");
u8g.drawStr( 07, 38, "Graphical LCD");
u8g.drawStr( 07, 58, "with Arduino");
}
void clearLCD(){
 u8g.firstPage();
 do {
 } while( u8g.nextPage() );
}
void setup(void) {
 // assign default color value
 if ( u8g.getMode() == U8G_MODE_R3G3B2 ) {
  u8g.setColorIndex(255);   // white
 }
 else if ( u8g.getMode() == U8G_MODE_GRAY2BIT ) {
  u8g.setColorIndex(3);     // max intensity
 }
 else if ( u8g.getMode() == U8G_MODE_BW ) {
  u8g.setColorIndex(1);     // pixel on
 }
 else if ( u8g.getMode() == U8G_MODE_HICOLOR ) {
  u8g.setHiColorByRGB(255,255,255);
 }
}
void loop(void) {
 // picture loop
 u8g.firstPage();
 do {
  u8g.drawFrame(1,2,126,62);
```

```
 draw();
} while( u8g.nextPage() );
delay(2000);
clearLCD();
u8g.firstPage();
do {
 u8g.drawFrame(1,2,126,62);
 next();
} while( u8g.nextPage() );
 delay(2000);
clearLCD();
u8g.firstPage();
do {
 picture();
} while( u8g.nextPage() );
 delay(3000);
clearLCD();
 // rebuild the picture after some delay
 delay(50);
}
```

4.AUTOMATIC PET FEEDER
USING ARDUINO

Today we are building an Arduino based Programmed Pet Feeder which can naturally serve nourishment to your pet auspicious. It has a DS3231 RTC (Real Time Clock) Module, which used to set time and date on which your pet ought to be given nourishment. In this way, by setting up the time as per your pet's eating plan, the gadget drop or fill the nourishment bowl consequently.

In this circuit, we are utilizing a 16*2 LCD to show the time utilizing DS3231 RTC Module with Arduino UNO. Likewise, a servo engine is utilized to pivot the compartments to give the nourishment and 4*4 lattice keypad to physically set up the ideal opportunity for sustaining the Pet. You can set the pivot point and holder opening term as indicated by the amount of nourishment you need to serve to your pet. The amount of nourishment may likewise rely on your pet whether it's a canine, feline or winged creature.

Material Required

- Arduino UNO
- 4*4 Matrix Keypad
- 16*2 LCD
- Push Button
- Servo Motor
- Resistor
- Connecting Wires
- Breadboard

Circuit Diagram

In this Arduino based Cat Feeder, for Getting Time as well as Date, we have utilized RTC Module. We have utilized the 4*4 Matrix Keypad to set the Pet's eating time physically with the assistance of 16x2 LCD. The Servo engine pivots the compartment and drop the nourishment on the time set by the client. The LCD is utilized for showing the Date and Time.

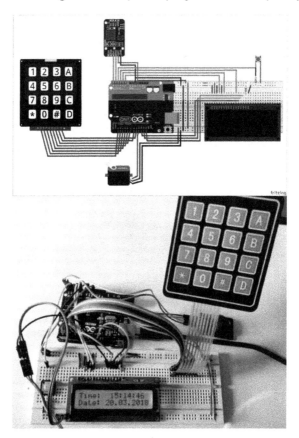

3D-Printed Pet Feeder Model

We have planned this Arduino Pet Feeder compartment utilizing the 3D-printer. You can likewise print a similar structure by downloading the records from here. The material utilized for printing this model is PLA. It has four Parts as appeared in the picture underneath:

Amass the four sections and interface the Servo Motor as appeared in the image underneath:

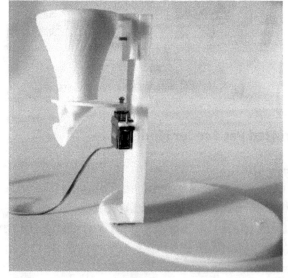

On the off chance that you are new to 3D printing here is the beginning aide. You can download the STL documents for this pet feeder here.

DS3231 RTC Module

DS3231 is a RTC module. It is utilized to keep up the date and time for the huge majority of the Electronics ventures. This module has its very own coin cell power supply utilizing which it keeps up the date and time notwithstanding when the principle power is evacuated or the MCU has experienced a hard reset. So once we set the date and time in this module it will monitor it generally. In our circuit, we are utilizing DS3231 to sustain the pet as indicated by the time, set up by the Pet's proprietor, similar to an alert. As, clock scopes to the set time, it works the servo engine to open the compartment door and the nourishment drops in the Pet's nourishment bowl.

Note: When utilizing this module just because you need to set the date and time. You can likewise utilize RTC IC DS1307 for perusing the time with Arduino.

Code and Explanation

Automatics Pet Feeder's whole Arduino Code is given underneath.

Arduino have default libraries for utilizing the Servo engine and LCD 16*2 with it. Be that as it may, for utilizing DS3231 RTC Module and 4*4 Matrix Keypad with the Arduino, you need to download and introduce the libraries. The download connect for both the libraries is given beneath:

- DS3231 RTC (Real Time Clock) Module Library

- 4*4 Matrix Keypad Library

In the beneath code, we are characterizing libraries, "#include <DS3231.h>" for RTC module, "#include <Servo.h>" for Servo Motor, "#include <LiquidCrystal.h>" for 16*2 LCD, and "#include <Keypad.h>" for 4*4 Matrix Keypad.

```
#include <DS3231.h>

#include <Servo.h>

#include <LiquidCrystal.h>
```

```
#include <Keypad.h>
```

In the beneath code, we are characterizing the keymap for the 4*4 network keypad and allotting the Arduino pins for the Row and Columns of keypad.

```
char keys[ROWS][COLS] = {

  {'1','2','3','A'},

  {'4','5','6','B'},

  {'7','8','9','C'},

  {'*','0','#','D'}

};

byte rowPins[ROWS] = { 2, 3, 4, 5 };

byte colPins[COLS] = { 6, 7, 8, 9 };
```

Here, we are making the keypad by utilizing the direction beneath in the code.

```
Keypad kpd = Keypad( makeKeymap(keys), rowPins, colPins, ROWS, COLS );
```

Appointing A4 and A5 Arduino pins to associate with SCL and SDA pins of DS3231. Likewise, doling out pins to the LCD and instating the Servo engine.

```
DS3231 rtc(A4, A5);

Servo servo_test;      //initialize a servo object for
the connected servo

LiquidCrystal lcd(A0, A1, A2, 11, 12, 13); // Creates
an LC object. Parameters: (rs, enable, d4, d5, d6, d7)
```

In the underneath code, we are pronouncing the t1 to t6, key, and exhibit r[6], and the feed.

```
int t1, t2, t3, t4, t5, t6;

boolean feed = true;

char key;

 int r[6];
```

In the underneath code, we are setting up every one of the segments for the beginning. Like in this code "servo_test.attach(10);" Servo is appended to the tenth stick of the Arduino. Characterizing A0, A1 and A2 as the Output Pin and introducing LCD and RTC module.

```
void setup()

{

  servo_test.attach(10);   // attach the signal pin of
  servo to pin9 of arduino

  rtc.begin();

  lcd.begin(16,2);

  servo_test.write(55);

  Serial.begin(9600);

  pinMode(A0, OUTPUT);

  pinMode(A1, OUTPUT);

  pinMode(A2, OUTPUT);

}
```

Presently, how the circle is working is the significant part to get it. At whatever point the Pushbutton is squeezed, it goes high means 1, which can be perused by "buttonPress = digitalRead(A3)". Presently it heads inside 'if' articulation and calles the 'setFeedingTime' work. At that point it looks at the continuous and the entered time by the client. On the off chance that the condition is genuine which means the continuous and the entered time is same, at that point the Servo engine pivots to and edge of 100 degree as well as after 0.4seconds of postpone it returns to its underlying position.

```
void loop() {

lcd.setCursor(0,0);

int buttonPress;

buttonPress = digitalRead(A3);

if(buttonPress==1)

 setFeedingTime();

 lcd.print("Time: ");

String t = "";

t = rtc.getTimeStr();

t1 = t.charAt(0)-48;

t2 = t.charAt(1)-48;
```

```
t3 = t.charAt(3)-48;

t4 = t.charAt(4)-48;

t5 = t.charAt(6)-48;

t6 = t.charAt(7)-48;

 lcd.print(rtc.getTimeStr());

 lcd.setCursor(0,1);

 lcd.print("Date: ");

 lcd.print(rtc.getDateStr());

if(t1==r[0] && t2==r[1] && t3==r[2] && t4==r[3]&&
t5<1 && t6<3 && feed==true)

{

 servo_test.write(100);      //command to rotate
the servo to the specified angle

  delay(400);

 servo_test.write(55);

 feed=false;
```

```
}

}
```

In the void setFeedingTime() work code, After squeezing the pushbutton we can enter the pet encouraging time, at that point we need to Press 'D' to spare that time. At the point when the spared time matches with constant then servo beginning pivoting.

```
void setFeedingTime()

{

  feed = true;

   int i=0;

  lcd.clear();

  lcd.setCursor(0,0);

  lcd.print("Set feeding Time");

  lcd.clear();

  lcd.print("HH:MM");

  lcd.setCursor(0,1);
```

```
while(1){

  key = kpd.getKey();

  char j;

if(key!=NO_KEY){

  lcd.setCursor(j,1);

  lcd.print(key);

  r[i] = key-48;

  i++;

  j++;

  if(j==2)

  {

    lcd.print(":");j++;

  }

  delay(500);

}
```

```
if(key == 'D')

{key=0; break;}

}

}
```

Working of the Automatic Pet Feeder

In the wake of transferring the code to the Arduino Uno, the time as well as date will be shown on the 16*2 LCD. When you squeezed the pushbutton it requests Pet's nourishing time and you need to enter the time utilizing the 4*4 lattice Keypad. Show will demonstrate the entered time and as you press 'D' it spares the time. At the point when the continuous and the Entered time matches, it turns the servo engine from its underlying position 55° to 100° and after a postponement again come back to its underlying position. In this manner, Servo engine is associated with the Food Container entryway, so as it moves, the door will open and some measure of nourishment falls in the bowl or plate. Following a defer 0.4 seconds Servo engine pivots again and close the entryway. The entire procedure finishes inside a couple of moments. This is the means by which your pet get the nourishment consequently on the time you entered.

Change time and degree as indicated by nourishment

Code

```
#include <DS3231.h>
#include <Servo.h>
#include <LiquidCrystal.h>
#include <Keypad.h>
const byte ROWS = 4; // Four rows
const byte COLS = 4; // Three columns
// Define the Keymap
char keys[ROWS][COLS] = {
 {'1','2','3','A'},
 {'4','5','6','B'},
 {'7','8','9','C'},
 {'*','0','#','D'}
};
// Connect keypad ROW0, ROW1, ROW2 and ROW3 to
these Arduino pins.
byte rowPins[ROWS] = { 2, 3, 4, 5 };
// Connect keypad COL0, COL1 and COL2 to these Ar-
```

```
duino pins.
byte colPins[COLS] = { 6, 7, 8, 9 };
// Create the Keypad
 Keypad kpd = Keypad( makeKeymap(keys), rowPins,
colPins, ROWS, COLS );
DS3231 rtc(A4, A5);
Servo servo_test;    //initialize a servo object for the
connected servo
LiquidCrystal lcd(A0, A1, A2, 11, 12, 13); // Creates an
LC object. Parameters: (rs, enable, d4, d5, d6, d7)
//int angle = 0;
// int potentio = A0;     // initialize the A0analog pin
for potentiometer
 int t1, t2, t3, t4, t5, t6;


boolean feed = true; // condition for alarm
 char key;
 int r[6];


 void setup()
{
  servo_test.attach(10);   // attach the signal pin of
servo to pin9 of arduino
 rtc.begin();
 lcd.begin(16,2);
 servo_test.write(55);
 Serial.begin(9600);
 pinMode(A0, OUTPUT);
```

```
pinMode(A1, OUTPUT);
pinMode(A2, OUTPUT);


}


void loop()
{
lcd.setCursor(0,0);
int buttonPress;
buttonPress = digitalRead(A3);
if (buttonPress==1)
setFeedingTime();

//Serial.println(buttonPress);
lcd.print("Time: ");
String t = "";
t = rtc.getTimeStr();
t1 = t.charAt(0)-48;
t2 = t.charAt(1)-48;
t3 = t.charAt(3)-48;
t4 = t.charAt(4)-48;
t5 = t.charAt(6)-48;
t6 = t.charAt(7)-48;


lcd.print(rtc.getTimeStr());
lcd.setCursor(0,1);
lcd.print("Date: ");
lcd.print(rtc.getDateStr());
```

```
 if (t1==r[0] && t2==r[1] && t3==r[2] && t4==r[3]&&
t5<1 && t6<3 && feed==true)
{
 servo_test.write(100);          //command to rotate
the servo to the specified angle
 delay(400);
 servo_test.write(55);
 feed=false;
}
}
void setFeedingTime()
{
 feed = true;
 int i=0;
lcd.clear();
lcd.setCursor(0,0);
lcd.print("Set feeding Time");
lcd.clear();
lcd.print("HH:MM");
lcd.setCursor(0,1);


 while(1){
 key = kpd.getKey();
 char j;


 if(key!=NO_KEY){
```

```
   lcd.setCursor(j,1);

   lcd.print(key);

  r[i] = key-48;
 i++;
 j++;
 if(j==2)
 {
  lcd.print(":");j++;
 }
 delay(500);
 }
if(key == 'D')
{key=0;break;}
 }
}
```

5.DIY ARDUINO INCLINOMETER USING MPU6050

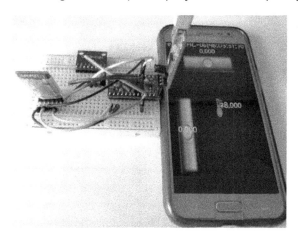

The MPU6050 is an IC 3-pivot accelerometer and a 3-hub spinner consolidated into one unit. It likewise houses a temperature sensor and a DCM to play an intricate errand. The MPU6050 is usually utilized in structure Drone and other remote robots like a self-adjusting robot. In this venture we will figure out how to utilize the MPU6050 is assembled an In-clinometer or Spirit Leveler. As we probably am aware an inclinometer is utilized to check if a surface is superbly leveled or not, they are accessible either as sprit bubble ones or as advanced meters. Here, we are going to assemble a Digital Inclinometer which can be checked utilizing an Android application. The purpose behind utilizing a remote presentation like a cell phone is that we can screen the qualities from MPU6050 without taking a gander at the equipment, this would come extremely convenient when the MPU6050 is set on an automaton or some other out of reach areas.

Materials Required:

- Advanced mobile phone

- MPU6050 Gyro Sensor

- Arduino Pro-small (5V)

- FTDI board

- HC-05 or HC-06 Bluetooth module

- Interfacing wires

- Breadboard

MPU6050 Gyro Sensor

Circuit Diagram:

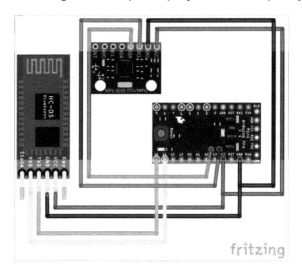

The total circuit chart for this Arduino Tilt Sensor Project is demonstrated as follows. It simply has just three segments and can be effectively worked over the breadboard.

The MPU6050 speaks with the assistance of I2C and thus the SDA stick is associated with the A4 stick of Arduino which is the SDA stick and the SCL stick is associated with the A5 stick of Arduino. The HC-06 Bluetooth Module works with the assistance of Serial correspondence consequently the Rx stick of Bluetooth is associated with stick D11 and the Tx stick of Bluetooth is associated with stick D10 of the Arduino. These stick D10 and D11 will be arranged as Serial stick by programming the Arduino. The HC-05 module and the MSP6050 module works on +5V and consequently they are controlled by the Vcc stick of the Arduino as appeared previously.

I utilized some breadboard interfacing wires and developed the set over a little breadboard. When the associations are done my board resembles this underneath.

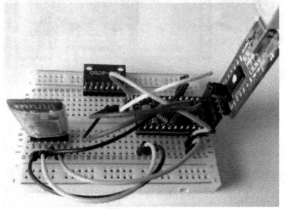

Powering your setup:

You can either control your circuit through the FTDI programming board as I have did, or utilize a 9V battery or 12V connector and associate it to the Raw stick of the Arduino expert smaller than normal. The Arduino Pro-scaled down has an in-manufactured voltage controller which would change over this outer voltage directed +5V.

FTDI Serial Adapter Module

Programming your Arduino:

When the equipment is prepared, we can begin programming our Arduino. As consistently the total code for this undertaking can be found at the base of this page. Be that as it may, to comprehend the undertaking better I have broken the code to little chinks and clarified them as steps beneath.

The initial step would be interfacing the MPU6050 with Arduino. For this venture we are going to utilize the library created by Korneliusz which can be downloaded from connection beneath

MPU6050 Liberty - Korneliusz Jarzebski

Download the ZIP record as well as add it to your Arduino IDE. At that point head on to File->Examples->Arduino_MPU6050_Master - > MPU6050_gyro_pitch_roll_yaw. This will open the model program that uses the library that we just downloaded. So click on transfer and trust that the program will be transferred to your Arduino Pro smaller than usual. When that is done open your sequential screen and set your baud rate to 115200 and check on the off chance that you are getting the accompanying.

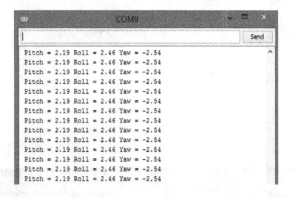

At first, all the three qualities will be as zero, yet as you move your breadboard you can watch these qualities getting changed. In the event that they change it implies your association is right, else check your associations. Take some time here notice how the three qualities Pitch Roll and Yaw differ as per the manner in which you tilt your sensor. On the off chance that you get confounded press the reset catch on the Arduino and the qualities will be instated to zero once more, at that point tilt the sensor one way and check which esteems are changing. The underneath picture will assist you with understanding better.

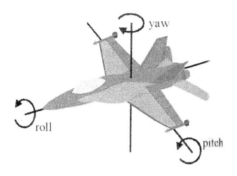

Out of these three parameters we are intrigued distinctly with regards to Roll and Pitch. The Roll worth will enlighten us regarding the tendency in X-pivot and the Pitch worth will inform us concerning the tendency in Y-Axis. Since we have comprehended the fundamentals lets really start programming the Arduino to peruse these qualities send it over to Arduino through Bluetooth. As forever how about we start by including every one of the libraries required for this venture

```
#include <Wire.h> //Lib for IIC communication

#include <MPU6050.h> //Lib for MPU6050
```

```
#include <SoftwareSerial.h>// import the serial li-
brary
```

At that point we introduce the product sequential for the Bluetooth module. This is conceivable due to the Software Serial library in Arduino, the IO pins can be modified to fill in as Serial pins. Here we are utilizing the computerized pins D10 as well as D11, where D10 id Rx as well as D11 is Tx.

```
SoftwareSerial BT(10, 11); // RX, TX
```

Pursued by that we instate the factors and articles required for the program and move onto the arrangement() work where we indicate the baud rate for Serial screen and Bluetooth. For HC-05 and HC-06 the baud rate is 9600 so it is obligatory to utilize the equivalent. At that point we check if the IIC transport of Arduino is associated with MPU6050 if not we print a notice message and stay there as long as the gadget is associated. From that point onward, we align the Gyro and set its limit esteems utilizing its individual capacities as demonstrated as follows.

```
void setup()

{
```

```
Serial.begin(115200);

BT.begin(9600); //start the Bluetooth communi-
cation at 9600 baudrate

// Initialize MPU6050

while(!mpu.begin(MPU6050_SCALE_2000DPS,
MPU6050_RANGE_2G))

{

  Serial.println("Could not find a valid MPU6050
sensor, check wiring!");

  delay(500);

}

mpu.calibrateGyro();  // Calibrate gyroscope dur-
ing start

mpu.setThreshold(3); //Controls the sensitivty

}
```

The line "mpu.calibrateGyro();" align the MPU6050 for the position it is as of now set at. This line can be called on various occasions inside the program at whatever point the MPU6050 should be aligned and all qualities are to be set to zero. "mpu.setThreshold(3);" this capacity controls how much the worth shifts for the development on sensor a too low worth will build the clamor so be cautious while tinkering with this.

Inside the void circle(), we over and over read the estimations of Gyroscope and Temperature sensor figure the estimation of pitch, roll and yaw, send it to the Bluetooth module. The accompanying two lines will peruse the crude Gyro esteems and the temperature esteem

```
Vector norm = mpu.readNormalizeGyro();

temp = mpu.readTemperature();
```

Next, we figure the pitch, roll, and yaw by increasing with time step and adding it up to the past qualities. A timeStep is only the interim between progressive readings.

```
pitch = pitch + norm.YAxis * timeStep;

roll = roll + norm.XAxis * timeStep;

yaw = yaw + norm.ZAxis * timeStep;
```

To comprehend time step better we should investigate the underneath line. This line is put to peruse the qualities from MPU6050 precisely at an interim of 10mS or 0.01 Second. So we pronounce the estimation of timeStep as 0.01. What's more, utilize the line underneath to hold the program if there if there is additional time left. (millis() – clock()) gives the time taken for the program to execute up until this point. We simply subtract it with 0.01 seconds and for the rest of the time we simply hold our program there utilizing the defer work.

```
delay((timeStep*1000) - (millis() - timer));
```

When we are finished perusing and figuring the qualities, we can send them over to our telephone by means of Bluetooth. However, there is a trick here. Bluetooth module that we are utilizing can send just 1 byte (8 bits) which enables us to send numbers just from 0 to 255. So we need to part our qualities and guide it inside this range. This is finished by the accompanying lines

```
if (roll>-100 && roll<100)

x = map (roll, -100, 100, 0, 100);

if (pitch>-100 && pitch<100)
```

```
y = map (pitch, -100, 100, 100, 200);

if (temp>0 && temp<50)

t = 200 + int(temp);
```

As you can make sense of it, the estimation of fold is mapped into 0 to 100 into the variable x and pitch is mapped to 100 to 200 into the variable y and temp is mapped into 200 or more into the variable t. We can utilize a similar data to recover the information from what we have sent. At last we compose these qualities through the Bluetooth utilizing the accompanying lines.

```
BT.write(x);

BT.write(y);

BT.write(t);
```

By any chance you have comprehended the total program, look down to examine the program and transfer it to the Arduino board.

Preparing the Android Application using Processing:

The android application for this Arduino Inclinometer was created utilizing the Processing IDE. This is particularly like Arduino and can be utilized to make framework application, Android application, website compositions and substantially more. We have just utilized preparing to build up a portion of our other cool tasks that are recorded beneath

- Ping Pong Game utilizing Arduino

- Advanced cell Controlled FM Radio utilizing Processing.

- Arduino Radar System utilizing Processing and Ultrasonic Sensor

Be that as it may, it is absurd to expect to clarify the total code on the best way to make this application. So you have two approaches over this. It is possible to download the APK record from the beneath connection and introduce the android application legitimately on your telephone. At the mean time look beneath to locate the total handling code and learn independent from anyone else how it functions

Android APK File for Arduino Inclinometer (Right Click and Save Link As...)

Note: The application as an issue of course just associates with Bluetooth gadgets named as "HC-06"

Understanding the Processing Code:

For the individuals who picked the later of under-standing the preparing code, I might want to clar-ify couple of significant focuses. The code requires Android method of handling to work which thus needs the Android SDK records. The establishment is somewhat cumbersome however it is all justified, even though all the trouble. Second, in case you are attempting to utilize this code given underneath, at that point you will require the accompanying ZIP record which contains the information document alongside the code

Preparing project ZIP record for Arduino Inclinometer

Inside the ZIP record, you can discover an organizer called information which comprises of the considerable number of pictures and different sources that will be stacked into the android application. The underneath line chooses to which name the Bluetooth ought to consequently interface with

```
bt.connectToDeviceByName("HC-06");
```

Inside the draw() work, the things will be executed over and over here we draw the pictures, show the content and quicken the bars dependent on the qualities structure the Bluetooth module. You can check what occurs inside each capacity by perusing the program.

```
void draw() //The infinite loop

{

background(0);

imageMode(CENTER);

image(logo,    width/2,    height/1.04,    width,
```

```
height/12);

  load_images();

  textfun();

  getval();

}
```

At long last, there is one increasingly significant thing to clarify, recall that we split the estimation of pitch, roll and temp to 0 to 255. So here we again take it back to ordinary qualities by switch mapping it to typical qualities.

```
if (info < 100 && info > 0)

  x  =  map(info,  0,  100,  -(width/1.5)/3,  +
(width/1.5)/3);//x = info;

  else if (info < 200 && info > 100)

  y  =  map(info,  100,  200,  -(width/4.5)/0.8,  +
(width/4.5)/0.8);//y = info;

  else if (info > 200)

  temp = info -200;
```

```
println(temp,x,y);
```

There are vastly improved approaches to get information from a Bluetooth module to telephone, yet since this is only a side interest venture we have disregarded them, you can burrow profound whenever intrigued.

Working of Arduino Inclinometer:

After you prepare with the Hardware and Application, it's an ideal opportunity to mess around with what we have fabricated. Transfer the Arduino Code to the board, you can likewise expel the remarks on Serial.println lines and check if the equipment is filling in true to form utilizing the sequential screen. Anyway, that is totally discretionary.

When the code is transferred, dispatch the Android application on your cell phone. The application ought to naturally interface with your HC-06 module and it will show "Associate with: HC-06" on the highest point of the application as demonstrated as follows.

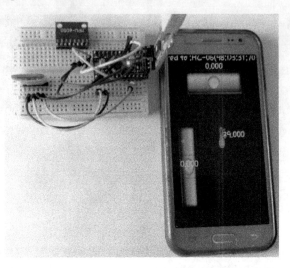

At first, every one of the qualities will be zero aside from the temperature esteem. This is on the grounds that the Arduino has adjusted the MPU-6050 for this situation as a kind of perspective, presently you can tilt the equipment and watch that the qualities on the versatile application are likewise changing alongside the movement. So now you can put the breadboard anyplace and check if the surface is consummately leveled.

Expectation you comprehended the task and picked up something helpful out of it. By any chance you have any uncertainty please utilize the remark segment beneath or the discussions to get it settled.

Code
/*

MPU6050 Librarey: **https://github.com/jarzebski/ Arduino-MPU6050** (c) 2014 by Korneliusz Jarzebski
*/

```
#include <Wire.h> //Lib for IIC communication
#include <MPU6050.h> //Lib for MPU6050
#include <SoftwareSerial.h>// import the serial library
SoftwareSerial BT(10, 11); // RX, TX
MPU6050 mpu;
unsigned long timer = 0;
unsigned long timer2 = 0;
float timeStep = 0.01;
float pitch = 0;
float roll = 0;
float yaw = 0;
float temp =0;
void setup()
{
 Serial.begin(115200);
  BT.begin(9600); //start the Bluetooth communication at 9600 baudrate
 // Initialize MPU6050
      while(!mpu.begin(MPU6050_SCALE_2000DPS, MPU6050_RANGE_2G))
 {
  Serial.println("Could not find a valid MPU6050 sensor, check wiring!");
  delay(500);
 }
```

```
  mpu.calibrateGyro();  // Calibrate gyroscope during
start
 mpu.setThreshold(3); //Controls the sensitivty
}
void loop()
{
 timer = millis();
 //Read Gyro and Temperature sensor values
 Vector norm = mpu.readNormalizeGyro();
 temp = mpu.readTemperature();
 // Calculate Pitch, Roll and Yaw
 pitch = pitch + norm.YAxis*timeStep;
 roll = roll + norm.XAxis*timeStep;
 yaw = yaw + norm.ZAxis*timeStep;
 // Print values
 Serial.print(" Pitch = ");
 Serial.print(pitch);
 Serial.print(" Roll = ");
 Serial.print(roll);
 Serial.print(" Yaw = ");
 Serial.print(yaw);
 Serial.print(" Temp = ");
 Serial.print(temp);
 Serial.println(" *C");
  delay((timeStep*1000) - (millis() - timer)); //makes
sure we read only at a an interval of 0.01 secounds
 if((millis()-timer2) > 200)
 send_BT();
```

```
}
void send_BT()
{
 int t;
 int x;
 int y;
 if(roll>-100 && roll<100)
 x = map (roll, -100, 100, 0, 100);
 if(pitch>-100 && pitch<100)
 y = map (pitch, -100, 100, 100, 200);
 if(temp>0 && temp<50)
 t = 200 + int(temp);


 BT.write(x);
 BT.write(y);
 BT.write(t);
 timer2 = millis();
}
```

6.ARDUINO ALCOHOL DETECTOR CIRCUIT BOARD

In this undertaking, we are gonna to Interface an Alcohol Sensor with Arduino. Here I have structured an Arduino Shield PCB utilizing EASYEDA online PCB test system and creator. Arduino Alcohol Detector will identify the liquor level in breath and by utilizing a few estimations in code we can ascertain the liquor level in breath or blood and can trigger some alert.

Components Required:

- Arduino UNO
- Alcohol detector Arduino shield from JLCPCB
- Alcohol Sensor (MQ3)
- Resistor 10K
- Resistor 1K
- 16x2 LCD
- Power Supply
- 10k POT
- LED

- LM358
- Burgstips
- Push button

Circuit Diagram and Explanation:

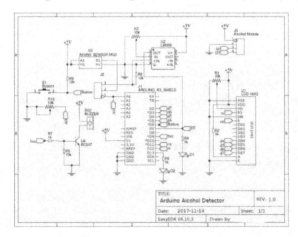

In this Arduino Alcohol Detector Shield we have utilized a MQ3 sensor to identify present liquor level in the breath. A 16x2 LCD is utilized for showing the PPM Value of liquor. Also, a LM358 IC for changing over liquor level sensor yield to advanced (this capacity is discretionary). A signal is additionally place for showing high liquor level.

Circuit Diagram for this Arduino Alcohol Sensor Project is given above. We have a comparator circuit for contrasting yield voltage of Alcohol Sensor and preset voltage (yield associated at stick D7). Liquor sensor yield is likewise associated at a simple stick of Arduino (A0). Ringer is associated at Pin D9. What's more, LCD associations are same as Arduino LCD models that are accessible in Arduino IDE (12, 11, 5, 4, 3, 2). A push catch likewise utilized here for beginning taking perusing from Alcohol Sensor associated at advanced stick D6 of Arduino. Remaining associations are appeared in the circuit graph.

Note: In the circuit, we have to short all the three stick of J2 header to figure PPM.

For planning Alcohol Detector Shield for Arduino we have utilized EasyEDA, in which first we have structured a Schematic and after that changed over that into the PCB design via Auto Routing highlight of EasyEDA. Complete Process is clarified underneath.

Calculations for Alcohol Level:

As indicated by MQ3 datasheet, liquor in clean air is

0.04 mg/L.

So we control the circuit and discover the yield voltage of MQ3 sensor in room air (I expect my room has clean air) so I got 0.60 voltage. It implies at the point when the sensor is giving 0 60v in the spotless air then liquor will be 0.04 mg/L.

Presently we can discover a multiplier by separating liquor by yield voltage in clean air and we get

Multiplier = 0.40/0.60

Multiplier = 0.67

Presently we have an equation for computing liquor (might be far away from the exact or real computation. These are not standard computations)

Alcohol = 0.67 * v .

Where v is the yield voltage of liquor sensor.

Note: This count isn't precise or standard.

Presently we know the least driving farthest point while drinking liquor is around 0.5mg/L. In any case, in our estimation, we are getting around 0.40 mg/L in clean air so we have set a limit of liquor while driving

0.80mg/L (only for Demonstration).

MQ3 Sensor:

MQ3 liquor gas sensor is made by utilizing SnO2 material which has less conductivity in clean air. At whatever point it comes close by liquor gas its beginnings leading profoundly as per the gas fixation. So client can detect the distinction of yield voltage utilizing any microcontroller and can recognize the nearness of Alcohol. This is ease and a reasonable sensor for some applications for liquor location. This sensor has a long life and great affectability. A portion of the applications that can be made by utilizing this sensor are Alcohol gas alert, compact liquor finder, gas cautions, Breathalyzer and so on.

Circuit and PCB Design using EasyEDA:

To plan this Arduino Alcohol Project Circuit, we have picked the online EDA apparatus called EasyEDA. I have recently utilized EasyEDA commonly and thought that it was exceptionally helpful to use since it has a decent accumulation of impressions and its open-source. Check here our everything the PCB ventures. In the wake of structuring the PCB, we can arrange the PCB tests by their minimal effort . They likewise offer part sourcing administration where they have an enormous load of electronic segments and clients can arrange their required segments alongside the PCB request.

While planning your circuits and PCBs, you can likewise make your circuit and PCB structures open with the goal that different clients can duplicate or alter them and can take profit by there, we have additionally made our entire Circuit and PCB formats open for this Arduino Alcohol Detector,

You can see any Layer (Top, Bottom, Topsilk, bottom-silk and so forth) of the PCB by choosing the layer structure the 'Layers' Window.

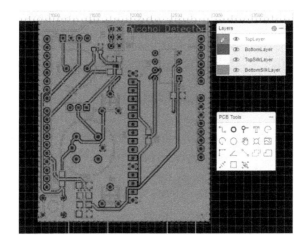

You can likewise see the PCB, how it will take care of creation utilizing the Photo View catch in EasyEDA:

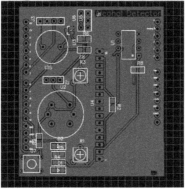

Calculating and Ordering Samples online:

In the wake of finishing the structure of this Arduino Alcohol Project PCB, you can arrange the PCB through . To arrange the PCB from JLCPCB, you need Gerber File. To download Gerber records of your PCB simply click the Fabrication Output catch in EasyEDA manager page, at that point download from the EasyEDA PCB request page.

Presently go to and click on Quote Now or Buy Now catch, at that point you can choose the quantity of PCBs you need to arrange, what number of copper layers you need, the PCB thickness, copper weight, and even the PCB shading, similar to the preview demonstrated as follows:

After you have chosen the majority of the choices, click "Spare to Cart" and afterward you will be taken to the page where you can transfer your Gerber File which we have downloaded from EasyEDA. Transfer your Gerber document and snap "Spare to Cart". Lastly click on Checkout Securely to finish your request, at that point you will get your PCBs a few days after the fact. They are manufacturing the PCB at low rate which is $2. Their assemble time is likewise extremely less which is 48 hours with DHL conveyance of 3-5 days, essentially you will get your PCBs inside seven days of requesting.

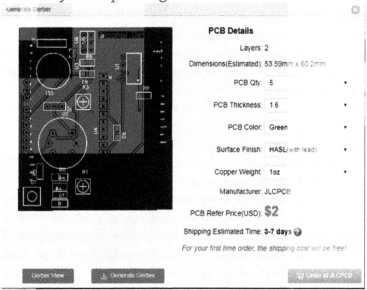

Following couple of long stretches of requesting PCB's I got the PCB tests in decent bundling as appeared in underneath pictures.

Furthermore, in the wake of getting these pieces I have fastened all the required parts over the PCB,

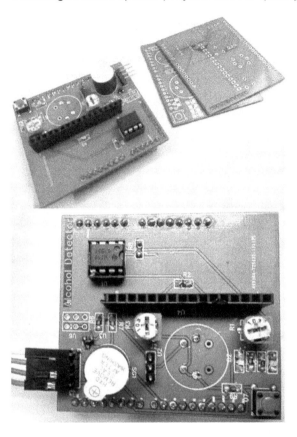

Presently we simply need to join LCD to the Shield and spot this Alcohol Detector Shield over the Arduino. Adjust the Pins of this Shield to the Arduino and solidly press it over the Arduino. Presently simply transfer the code to the Arduino and power on the circuit and you are finished! Your Alcohol Detector is prepared to test.

Code

```
#include <LiquidCrystal.h>
LiquidCrystal lcd(12,11,5,4,3,2);
#define sensor A0
#define led 13
#define buz 9
void setup()
{
 Serial.begin(9600);
 lcd.begin(16,2);
 lcd.print("Alcohol Detector");
 lcd.setCursor(0,1);
 lcd.print(" Hello world");
 delay(2000);
 pinMode(sensor, INPUT);
 pinMode(buz, OUTPUT);
 pinMode(led, OUTPUT);
 lcd.clear();
}
void loop()
```

```
{
 float adcValue=0;
 for(int i=0;i<10;i++)
 {
  adcValue+=analogRead(sensor);
  delay(10);
 }
  float v=(adcValue/10)*(5.0/1024.0);
  float mgL=0.67*v;
  Serial.print("BAC:");
  Serial.print(mgL);
  Serial.print(" mg/L");
  lcd.setCursor(0,0);
  lcd.print("BAC: ");
  lcd.print(mgL,4);
  lcd.print(" mg/L    ");
  lcd.setCursor(0,1);
  if(mgL > 0.8)
  {
   lcd.print("Drunk ");
   Serial.println("  Drunk");
   digitalWrite(buz,HIGH);
   digitalWrite(led,HIGH);
  }
  else
  {
   lcd.print("Normal ");
   Serial.println("  Normal");
   digitalWrite(buz,LOW);
   digitalWrite(led,LOW);
```

```
  }
  delay(100);


}
```

7.INTERFACING JOYSTICK
WITH ARDUINO

Interfacing Joystick with Arduino

The primary thing that comes in our mind tuning in to the word Joystick is the game controller. Truly, it's actually the equivalent and can be utilized for gaming reason. Aside from gaming, it has numerous different applications in DIY hardware. This joystick is only a blend of two potentiometers for X and Y plane individually. It peruses the voltage through the potentiometer and gives simple incentive to the Arduino, and the simple worth changes as we move the joystick shaft (which is essentially the potentiometer pointer).

Here, we are interfacing Joystick with Arduino basically by controlling four LEDs according to the development of the Joystick. We have put 4 LEDs so that it speaks to the bearing of the joystick shaft development. This joystick likewise has a push catch which can be utilized for different purposes or can be left inactive. A solitary LED is likewise appended to the switch of the joystick, as the joystick catch squeezed that solitary LED will turn ON.

Material Required

- Arduino UNO
- Joystick Module
- LEDs-5
- Connecting wires
- Resistor: 100ohm-3
- Breadboard

Circuit Diagram

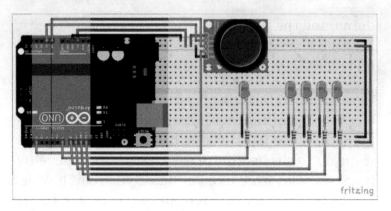

Joystick Module

Joysticks are accessible in various shapes as well as sizes. A run of the mill Joystick module is appeared in the figure beneath. This Joystick module regularly gives Analog Outputs and the yield voltages given by this module continue altering as per the course wherein we move it. What's more, we can get the bearing of development by translating these voltage changes utilizing some microcontroller. Already we interfaced Joystick with AVR and Raspberry Pi.

This joystick module has 2 tomahawks as should be obvious. They are X-pivot and Y-hub. Every pivot of JOYSTICK is mounted to a potentiometer or pot. The midpoints of these pots are driven out as Rx and Ry. So Rx and Ry are variable focuses to these pots. At the point when the Joystick is in backup, Rx and Ry go about as a voltage divider.

At the point when the joystick is moved along the even hub, the voltage at Rx stick changes. Essentially, when it is moved along the vertical pivot, the voltage at Ry stick changes. So we have four bearings of Joystick on two ADC yields. At the point when the stick is moved, the voltage on each stick goes high or low contingent upon course.

Here, we are associating this Joystick module with the Arduino UNO which accompanies an inbuilt ADC system. Get familiar with utilizing Arduino's ADC.

Code and Explanation

Complete Arduino Code is referenced toward the end.

In beneath code, we have characterized X and Y pivot of the Joystick module for simple stick A0 and A1 individually.

```
#define joyX A0

#define joyY A1
```

Presently, in the beneath code, we are instating PIN 2 of Arduino for the Switch (drive catch) of the Joystick module and the estimation of buttonstate and buttonstate1 will be 0 toward the beginning.

```
int button=2;

int buttonState = 0;

int buttonState1 = 0;
```

In the underneath code, we are setting up the baud rate to 9600 and characterized Pin 7 as a yield stick and catch stick as an info Pin. At first, the catch stick will stay high until the Switch will press.

```
void setup() {
```

```
pinMode(7,OUTPUT);

pinMode(button,INPUT);

digitalWrite(button, HIGH);

Serial.begin(9600);

}
```

Here, in this code we are perusing the qualities from the simple stick A0 and A1 and printing sequentially.

```
int xValue = analogRead(joyX);

int yValue = analogRead(joyY);

Serial.print(xValue);

Serial.print("\t");

Serial.println(yValue);
```

The conditions, for turning LED on and off according to the development of the Joystick shaft, are characterized in the code underneath. Here we are simply taking simple estimations of voltage at stick A0 as well as A1 of Arduino. These simple qualities will change as we move the joystick and LED will shine as per development of joystick.

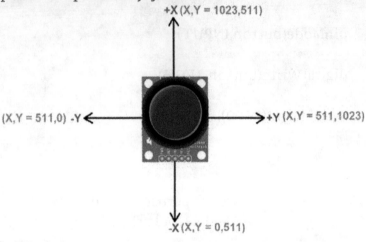

This condition is for development of Joystick shaft in - Y hub bearing

```
if (xValue>=0 && yValue<=10){

   digitalWrite(10, HIGH);

}

else{digitalWrite(10, LOW);}
```

This condition is for development of Joystick shaft in - X hub bearing

```
if (xValue<=10 && yValue>=500){

  digitalWrite(11, HIGH);

}

else{digitalWrite(11, LOW);}
```

This condition is for development of Joystick shaft in +X hub bearing

```
if (xValue>=1020 && yValue>=500){

  digitalWrite(9, HIGH);

}

else{digitalWrite(9, LOW);}
```

This condition is for development of Joystick shaft in +Y hub bearing

```
if (xValue>=500 && yValue>=1020){

  digitalWrite(8, HIGH);
```

```
}

else{digitalWrite(8, LOW);}
```

When we move the joystick shaft askew then one position come when the simple estimation of X and Y will be 1023 and 1023 individually, both Pin 9 and Pin 8 LED will gleam. Since it fulfills the state of the LED. Along these lines, for expelling that confuse we have given a condition that in case the estimation of (X, Y) is (1023, 1023) at that point both the LED stay in OFF condition

```
if(xValue>=1020 && yValue>=1020) {

    digitalWrite(9, LOW);

    digitalWrite(8, LOW);

}
```

The underneath condition is utilized to work the LED associated with the Pushbutton Switch. As we press the Joystick switch the LED will turn ON and hook until the catch discharge. Its discretionary to utilize the Push catch switch on Joystick module.

```
if(buttonState == LOW) {
```

```
Serial.println("Switch = High");

digitalWrite(7, HIGH);

}

else{digitalWrite(7, LOW);}
```

Controlling LEDs using Joystick with Arduino

In the wake of transferring the code to the Arduino and interface the segments according to the circuit graph, we would now be able to control the LEDs with Joystick. We can turn ON the four LEDs toward every path according to the Joystick shaft development. The Joystick is having two potentiometer inside it, one is for X-hub development and another is for Y-pivot development. Every potentiometer is getting 5v from the Arduino. So as we move the joystick, the voltage worth will change and the simple incentive at Analog pins A0 as well as A1 will likewise change.

In this way, from the Arduino, we are perusing the simple incentive for X and Y hub and turning ON the LEDs according to the pivot development of the Joystick. A push catch switch on Joystick module is utilized to control the single LED in the circuit .

Code

```
#define joyX A0
#define joyY A1
int button=2;
int buttonState = 0;
int buttonState1 = 0;
void setup() {
 pinMode(7,OUTPUT);
 pinMode(button,INPUT);
 digitalWrite(button, HIGH);
 Serial.begin(9600);
}


void loop() {
 int xValue = analogRead(joyX);
 int yValue = analogRead(joyY);


  Serial.print(xValue);
 Serial.print("\t");
 Serial.println(yValue);
```

```
buttonState = digitalRead(button);
Serial.println(buttonState);
if (xValue>=0 && yValue<=10)
{
  digitalWrite(10, HIGH);
}
else{digitalWrite(10, LOW);}
if (xValue<=10 && yValue>=500)
{
  digitalWrite(11, HIGH);
}
else{digitalWrite(11, LOW);}
if (xValue>=1020 && yValue>=500)
{
  digitalWrite(9, HIGH);
}
else{digitalWrite(9, LOW);}
if (xValue>=500 && yValue>=1020)
{
  digitalWrite(8, HIGH);
}
else{digitalWrite(8, LOW);}
if (xValue>=1020 && yValue>=1020)
{
  digitalWrite(9, LOW);
  digitalWrite(8, LOW);
}
if (buttonState == LOW)
```

```
{
 Serial.println("Switch = High");
 digitalWrite(7, HIGH);
}
else{digitalWrite(7, LOW);}
buttonState1 = digitalRead(7);
Serial.println(buttonState1);
delay(50);
}
```

8.ARDUINO LIGHT SENSOR CIRCUIT USING LDR

Arduino Light Sensor Circuit using LDR

We as a whole need our home machines to be controlled naturally dependent on certain conditions and that is called Home mechanization. Today we are going to control the light based of dimness outside, the light turns ON consequently when it is dull outside and turns off when it gets brilliant. For this, we require a light sensor to identify the light condition as well as some hardware to control the Light sensor. It resembles Dark and light Detector circuit yet this time we are utilizing Arduino to deal with light.

In this circuit, we are making a Light Sensor utilizing LDR with Arduino to control a bulb/CFL according to light state of the room or outside territory.

Material Required

- Breadboard

- Arduino UNO

- Resistor (100k-1; 330ohm-1)

- LDR

- Hand-off module - 5v

- Driven - 1

- Interfacing wires

- Bulb/CFL

Circuit Diagram

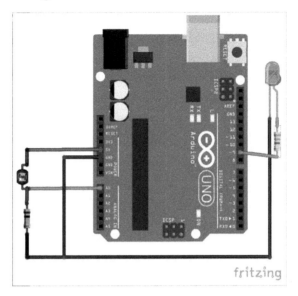

LDR

LDR is Light Dependent Resistor. LDRs are produced using semiconductor materials to empower them to have their light-touchy properties. There are numerous sorts however one material is well known and it is cadmium sulfide (CdS). These LDRs or PHOTO RESISTORS takes a shot at the standard of "Photograph Conductivity". Presently what this rule says is, at whatever point light falls on the outside of the LDR (for this situation) the conductance of the component increments or as it were, the obstruction of the LDR falls when the light falls on the outside of the

LDR. This property of the abatement in opposition for the LDR is accomplished on the grounds that it is a property of semiconductor material utilized superficially.

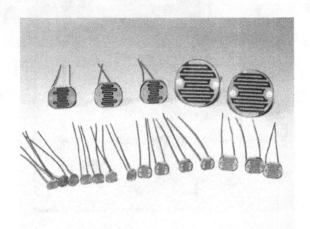

We recently made numerous Circuits utilizing LDR, which use LDR to computerize the lights as indicated by prerequisite.

Working of LDR controlled LED using Arduino

According to the circuit graph, we have made a voltage divider circuit utilizing LDR and 100k resistor. The voltage divider yield is feed to the simple stick of the Arduino. The simple Pin detects the voltage and gives some simple incentive to Arduino. The simple worth changes as per the opposition of LDR. In this way, as the light falls on the LDR its opposition get diminished and subsequently the voltage worth increment.

Power of light ? - Resistance? - Voltage at simple pin? - Light turns ON

According to the Arduino code, if the simple worth falls underneath 700 we consider it as dim and the light turns ON. In the event that the worth comes over 700 we consider it as brilliant and the light turns OFF.

Code Explanation:

Complete Arduino Code is given toward the finish of this undertaking.

Here, we are characterizing the Pins for Relay, LED and LDR.

```
#define relay 10

int LED = 9;

int LDR = A0;
```

Setting up the LED and Relay as Output stick, and LDR as info stick.

```
pinMode(LED, OUTPUT);
```

```
pinMode(relay, OUTPUT);

pinMode(LDR, INPUT);
```

Perusing the voltage simple incentive through the A0 stick of the Arduino. This simple Voltage will be expanded or diminished by the opposition of LDR.

```
int LDRValue = analogRead(LDR);
```

Giving the condition for dim and brilliant. In the event that the worth is under 700, at that point it is dull and the LED or Light turns ON. In case the worth is more prominent than 700, at that point it is brilliant and the LED or light turns OFF.

```
if (LDRValue <= 700)

{

digitalWrite(LED, HIGH);

digitalWrite(relay, HIGH);

Serial.println("It's Dark Outside; Lights status: ON");

}
```

```
Else

{

digitalWrite(LED, LOW);

digitalWrite(relay, LOW);

Serial.println("It's Bright Outside; Lights status: OFF");

}
```

Controlling Relay using LDR with Arduino

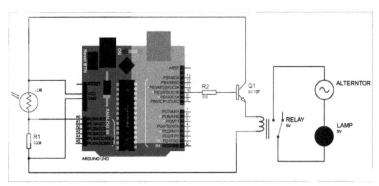

Rather than controlling a LED by the brilliance and dimness, we can control our home lights or any electrical hardware. We should simply interface a transfer module and set the parameter to kill ON and the any AC apparatus as indicated by the power of the light. In the event that the worth falls beneath 700,

137

which means it Dark, at that point the transfer works and the lights turns ON. On the off chance that the worth is more prominent than 700, which means its day or brilliant, at that point the transfer won't work and the lights stay OFF. Study hand-off here and how to associate an AC machine to transfer.

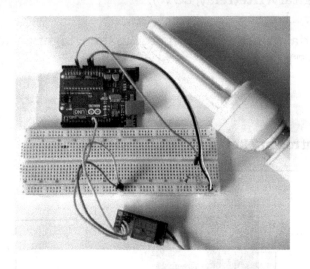

Additionally, check:

Programmed Street Light Controller Circuit Using Relay and LDR

Programmed Staircase Light

Raspberry Pi Emergency Light

Code

```
#define relay 10
int LED = 9;
int LDR = A0;
void setup()
{
Serial.begin(9600);
pinMode(LED, OUTPUT);
pinMode(relay, OUTPUT);
pinMode(LDR, INPUT);
}
void loop() {
int LDRValue = analogRead(LDR);
Serial.print("sensor = ");
Serial.print(LDRValue);
if (LDRValue <= 700)
{
digitalWrite(LED, HIGH);
digitalWrite(relay, HIGH);
Serial.println("It's Dark Outside; Lights status: ON");
}
else
{
digitalWrite(LED, LOW);
digitalWrite(relay, LOW);
Serial.println("It's Bright Outside; Lights status: OFF");
}
}
```

9.ARDUINO OHM METER

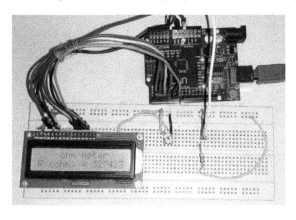

We think that its hard to peruse shading codes on resistors to discover its opposition. So as to conquer the trouble of finding the obstruction esteem, we are going to manufacture a straightforward Ohm Meter utilizing Arduino. The essential rule behind this venture is a Voltage Divider Network. The estimation of the obscure obstruction is shown on 16*2 LCD show. This venture likewise fills in as 16*2 LCD show interfacing with Arduino.

Components Required:

- Arduino Uno
- Potentiometer (1 kilo Ohm)
- 16*2 LCD display
- Breadboard
- Resistors
- Jumper wires

Circuit Diagram:

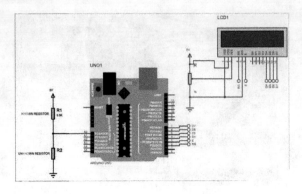

Arduino Uno:

Arduino Uno is an open source microcontroller board dependent on ATmega328p microcontroller. It has 14 advanced pins (out of which 6 pins can be utilized as PWM yields), 6 simple contributions, on board voltage controllers and so on. Arduino Uno has 32KB of blaze memory, 2KB of SRAM and 1KB of EEPROM. It works at the clock recurrence of 16MHz. Arduino Uno bolsters Serial , I2C , SPI correspondence for speaking with different gadgets. The table beneath demonstrates the specialized detail of Arduino Uno.

Microcontroller	ATmega328p
Operating voltage	5V
Input Voltage	7-12V (recommended)
Digital I/O pins	14
Analog pins	6

Flash memory	32KB
SRAM	2KB
EEPROM	1KB
Clock speed	16MHz

16x2 LCD:

16*2 LCD is a broadly utilized presentation for installed applications. Here is the short clarification about pins and working of 16*2 LCD show. There are two significant registers inside the LCD. They are information register and direction register. Direction register is utilized to send directions, for example, clear show, cursor at home and so on., information register is utilized to send information which is to be shown on 16*2 LCD. Beneath table demonstrates the stick depiction of 16*2 lcd.

Pin	Symbol	I/O	Description
1	Vss	-	Ground
2	Vdd	-	+5V power supply
3	Vee	-	Power supply to control contrast
4	RS	I	RS=0 for command register , RS=1 for data register

5	RW	I	R/W=0 for write , R/W=1 for read
6	E	I/O	Enable
7	D0	I/O	8-bit data bus(LSB)
8	D1	I/O	8-bit data bus
9	D2	I/O	8-bit data bus
10	D3	I/O	8-bit data bus
11	D4	I/O	8-bit data bus
12	D5	I/O	8-bit data bus
13	D6	I/O	8-bit data bus
14	D7	I/O	8-bit data bus(MSB)
15	A	-	+5V for backlight
16	K	-	Ground

Concept of Resistance Color Code:

To recognize the estimation of the opposition we can utilize the beneath recipe.

$$R= \{ (AB*10^c)\Omega \pm T\% \}$$

Where

A = Value of the shading in the primary band.

B = Value of the shading in the subsequent band.

C = Value of the shading in the third band.

T = Value of the shading in the fourth band.

The table underneath demonstrates the shading code of resistors.

Color	Numerical value of the color	Multiplication factor(10^c)	Tolerance value(T)
Black	0	10^0	-
Brown	1	10^1	± 1%
Red	2	10^2	± 2%
Orange	3	10^3	-
Yellow	4	10^4	-
Green	5	10^5	-
Blue	6	10^6	-
Violet	7	10^7	-
Gray	8	10^8	-
White	9	10^9	-
Gold	-	10^{-1}	± 5%
Silver	-	10^{-2}	± 10%
No band	-	-	± 20%

For instance, if the shading codes are Brown – Green – Red – Silver, the estimation of obstruction is determined as,

Brown = 1

Green = 5

Red = 2

Silver = ± 10%

From the initial three groups, R = AB*10c

$R = 15 * 10^{+2}$

R = 1500 Ω

Fourth band demonstrates resilience of ± 10%

10% of 1500 = 150

For + 10 percent, the value is 1500 + 150 = 1650Ω

For - 10 percent, the value is 1500 -150 = 1350Ω

In this way the genuine opposition worth can be anyplace between 1350? to 1650?.

To make it increasingly advantageous here is the Resistance Color Code Calculator where you just need enter the shade of rings on resistor and you will get the opposition esteem.

Calculating Resistance using Arduino Ohm Meter:

The working of this Resistance Meter is exceptionally basic and can be clarified utilizing a basic voltage divider system demonstrated as follows.

From the voltage divider system of resistors R1 as well as R2,

$$Vout = Vin * R2 / (R1 + R2)$$

From the above condition, we can conclude the estimation of R2 as

$$R2 = Vout * R1 / (Vin - Vout)$$

Where R1 = known obstruction

R2 = Unknown obstruction

Vin = voltage created at the 5V stick of Arduino

Vout = voltage at R2 concerning ground.

Note: the estimation of known obstruction (R1) picked is 3.3KO, yet the clients ought to supplant it with the opposition estimation of resistor they have picked.

So on the off chance that we get the estimation of voltage crosswise over obscure obstruction (Vout), we can without much of a stretch ascertain the obscure opposition R2. Here we have perused the voltage esteem Vout utilizing the simple stick A0 (see the circuit chart) and changed over those computerized qualities (0 - 1023) into voltage as clarified in Code underneath.

In case the estimation of the realized Resistance is far more prominent or littler than the obscure opposition the blunder will be more. So it is encouraged to keep the realized opposition esteem closer to the obscure obstruction.

Code explanation:

In this piece of the code, we will characterize the pins

on which 16*2 LCD show is associated with Arduino. RS stick of 16*2 lcd is associated with computerized stick 2 of arduino. Empower stick of 16*2 lcd is associated with computerized stick 3 of Arduino. Information pins (D4-D7) of 16*2 lcd is associated with advanced pins four,five,six,seven of Arduino.

```
LiquidCrystal lcd(2,3,4,5,6,7); //rs,e,d4,d5,d6,d7
```

In this piece of the code, we are characterizing a few factors that are utilized in the program. Vin is the voltage given by 5V stick of arduino. Vout is the voltage at resistor R2 as for ground.

R1 is the estimation of known obstruction. R2 is the estimation of obscure obstruction.

```
int Vin=5;     //voltage at 5V pin of arduino

float Vout=0;   //voltage at A0 pin of arduino

float R1=3300;  //value of known resistance

float R2=0;     //value of unknown resistance
```

In this piece of the code, we will introduce 16*2 lcd show. The directions are given to 16*2 lcd show for various settings, for example, clear screen, show on cursor squinting and so on.

```
lcd.begin(16,2);
```

In this piece of the code, the simple voltage at the resistor R2 (A0 stick) is changed over to advanced worth (0 to 1023) and put away in a variable.

```
a2d_data = analogRead(A0);
```

In this piece of the code, the advanced worth (0 to 1023) is changed over into voltage for further figurings.

```
buffer=a2d_data*Vin;

Vout=(buffer)/1024.0;
```

The Arduino Uno ADC is of 10-piece goals (so the whole number qualities from $0 - 2^{10} = 1024$ qualities). This implies it will guide input voltages somewhere in the range of 0 and 5 volts into whole number qualities somewhere in the range of 0 and 1023. So on the off chance that we duplicate info anlogValue to (5/1024), at that point we get the computerized estimation of information voltage. Learn here how to utilize ADC contribution to Arduino.

In this piece of the code, the genuine estimation of obscure obstruction is determined utilizing the strategy as clarified previously.

```
buffer=Vout/(Vin-Vout);

R2=R1*buffer;
```

In this piece of the code, the estimation of the obscure obstruction is imprinted on 16*2 lcd show.

```
lcd.setCursor(4,0);

lcd.print("ohm meter");

lcd.setCursor(0,1);

lcd.print("R(ohm) = ");

lcd.print(R2);
```

Without lot of a stretch we can compute the obstruction of an obscure resistor utilizing Arduino. Additionally, check:

- Arduino Frequency Meter

- Arduino Capacitance Meter

Code

```
#include<LiquidCrystal.h>
LiquidCrystal lcd(2,3,4,5,6,7); //rs,e,d4,d5,d6,d7
int Vin=5;    //voltage at 5V pin of arduino
float Vout=0;  //voltage at A0 pin of arduino
float R1=3300;  //value of known resistance
float R2=0;    //value of unknown resistance
int a2d_data=0;
float buffer=0;
void setup()
{
lcd.begin(16,2);
}
void loop()
{
 a2d_data=analogRead(A0);
 if(a2d_data)
 {
  buffer=a2d_data*Vin;
  Vout=(buffer)/1024.0;
  buffer=Vout/(Vin-Vout);
  R2=R1*buffer;
  lcd.setCursor(4,0);
  lcd.print("ohm meter");
  lcd.setCursor(0,1);
  lcd.print("R(ohm) = ");
```

```
lcd.print(R2);

  delay(1000);
 }
}
```

10.MPU6050 GYRO SENSOR INTERFACING WITH ARDUINO

MPU6050 sensor has numerous capacities over the single chip. It comprises a MEMS accelerometer, a MEMS gyro, and temperature sensor. This module is precise while changing over simple qualities to computerized on the grounds that it has a 16bit simple to advanced converter equipment for each channel. This module is fit to catch x, y and z channel simultaneously. It has an I2C interface to speak with the host controller. This MPU6050 module is a reduced chip having both accelerometer and gyro. This is a helpful gadget for some, applications like automatons, robots, movement sensors. It is additionally called Gyroscope or Triple pivot accelerometer.

Here we are gonna to interface this MPU6050 Gyroscope with Arduino and demonstrating the qualities over 16x2 LCD.

Required Components:

- Power supply
- MPU-6050
- Arduino Uno
- Jumper wire
- 10K POT
- USB cable
- Breadboard

MPU6050 Gyro Sensor:

MPU-6050 is a 8 stick 6 hub gyro and accelerometer in a solitary chip. This module chips away at I2C sequential correspondence as a matter of course however it tends to be designed for SPI interface by arranging it register. For I2C this has SDA and SCL lines. Practically every one of the pins are multifunctioning yet here we are continuing just with I2C mode pins.

Pin Configuration:

Vcc:- this stick is utilized for driving the MPU6050 module regarding ground

GND:- this is ground stick

SDA:- SDA stick is utilized for information among controller and mpu6050 module

SCL:- SCL stick is utilized for clock input

XDA:- This is sensor I2C SDA Data line for arranging and perusing from outer sensors ((discretionary) not utilized for our situation)

XCL:- This is sensor I2C SCL clock line for arranging and perusing from outer sensors ((discretionary) not utilized for our situation)

ADO:- I2C Slave Address LSB (not appropriate for our situation)

INT:- Interrupt stick for sign of information prepared.

Description:

In this article, we are indicating temperature, gyro and accelerometer readings over LCD utilizing MPU6050 with Arduino. This module gives us column esteems and standardized qualities in yield however line esteems are not steady so here we have demonstrating standardized qualities over LCD.In case you simply need accelerometer esteem, you can likewise utilize Accelerometer ADXL335 with Arduino.

In this venture, we have first demonstrated a temperature esteem over LCD and following 10 seconds we show gyro esteems and following 10 seconds we have accelerometer readings as appeared in the pictures underneath:

Circuit Diagram and Explanation:

The circuit graph, for interfacing MPU6050 with Arduino, is exceptionally straightforward here we have utilized a LCD and MPU6050. What's more, here we have utilized a workstation USB power supply. A 10k pot is utilized for controlling the brilliance of the LCD. Regarding MPU6050, we have completed 5 associations in which we have associated the 3.3v power supply and ground of MPU6050 to the 3.3v and ground of Arduino. SCL and SDA pins of MPU6050 is associated with Arduino's A4 and A5 stick. Furthermore, INT stick of MPU6050 is associated with intrude on 0 of Arduino (D2). LCD's RS, RW as well as EN are straightforwardly associated with 8, gnd as well as 9 of Arduino. Information stick are straightforwardly associated with computerized stick number 10, 11, 12 and 13.

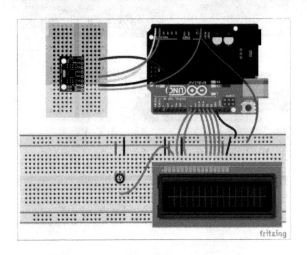

Programming Explanation:

Programming part is likewise simple for this venture. Here we have utilized this MPU6050 library to interface it with Arduino. So most importantly, we have to download the MPU6050 library from GitHub and introduce it in Arduino IDE.

After it, we can discover model codes in the model. The client may test that code by legitimately transferring them to Arduino and can see esteems over sequential screen. Or on the other hand the client may utilize our code given toward the finish of the article to show esteems over LCD and sequential screen also.

In coding, we have incorporated some required libraries like MPU6050 and LCD.

```
#include<LiquidCrystal.h>

LiquidCrystal lcd(8,9,10,11,12,13);

#include <Wire.h>

#include <MPU6050.h>
```

In arrangement work, we introduce the two gadgets and compose welcome message over LCD

```
void setup()

{

  lcd.begin(16,2);

  lcd.createChar(0, degree);

  Serial.begin(9600);
```

```
Serial.println("Initialize MPU6050");

while(!mpu.begin(MPU6050_SCALE_2000DPS,
MPU6050_RANGE_2G))

{

  lcd.clear();

  lcd.print("Device not Found");

  Serial.println("Could not find a valid MPU6050
sensor, check wiring!");

  delay(500);

}

count=0;

mpu.calibrateGyro();

mpu.setThreshold(3);
```

In circle Function, we have called three capacities in each 10seconds for showing temperature, gyro, and accelerometer perusing on LCD. These three capacities are tempShow, gyroShow and accelShow, you can check those capacities in the total Arduino code given toward the finish of this article:

```
void loop()

{

  lcd.clear();

  lcd.print("Temperature");

  long st=millis();

  Serial.println("Temperature");

  while(millis()<st+period)

  {

    lcd.setCursor(0,1);

    tempShow();

  }

  lcd.clear();

  lcd.print("Gyro");

  delay(2000);
```

```
st=millis();

Serial.println("Gyro");

while(millis()<st+period)

{

  lcd.setCursor(0,1);

  gyroShow();

}

lcd.clear();

lcd.print("Accelerometer");

delay(2000);

st=millis();
```

MPU6050 gyro and accelerometer both are utilized to recognize the position and direction of any gadget. Gyro uses earth gravity to decide the x,y and z-hub positions and accelerometer recognizes dependent on the pace of the difference in development. We previously utilized the accelerometer with Arduino in a large number of our activities like:

- Accelerometer Based Hand Gesture Controlled Robot

- Arduino Based Vehicle Accident Alert System

- Seismic tremor Detector Alarm utilizing Arduino

Code

```
#include<LiquidCrystal.h>
LiquidCrystal lcd(8,9,10,11,12,13);
#include <Wire.h>
#include <MPU6050.h>
#define period 10000
MPU6050 mpu;
int count=0;
char okFlag=0;
byte degree[8] = {
0b00000,
0b00110,
0b01111,
0b00110,
0b00000,
0b00000,
0b00000,
0b00000
};
void setup()
```

```
{
 lcd.begin(16,2);
 lcd.createChar(0, degree);
 Serial.begin(9600);
 Serial.println("Initialize MPU6050");
       while(!mpu.begin(MPU6050_SCALE_2000DPS,
MPU6050_RANGE_2G))
 {
  lcd.clear();
  lcd.print("Device not Found");
   Serial.println("Could not find a valid MPU6050 sen-
sor, check wiring!");
  delay(500);
 }
 count=0;
 mpu.calibrateGyro();
 mpu.setThreshold(3);


  lcd.clear();
 lcd.print("MPU6050 Interface");
 lcd.setCursor(0,1);
 lcd.print(" Hello world");
 delay(2000);
 lcd.clear();
}
void loop()
{
  lcd.clear();
  lcd.print("Temperature");
```

```
long st=millis();
Serial.println("Temperature");
while(millis()<st+period)
{
 lcd.setCursor(0,1);
 tempShow();
}


  lcd.clear();
lcd.print("Gyro");
delay(2000);
st=millis();
Serial.println("Gyro");
while(millis()<st+period)
{
 lcd.setCursor(0,1);
 gyroShow();
}
lcd.clear();
lcd.print("Accelerometer");
delay(2000);
st=millis();
Serial.println("Accelerometer");
while(millis()<st+period)
{
 lcd.setCursor(0,1);
 accelShow();
}
}
```

```
void tempShow()
{
  float temp = mpu.readTemperature();
  Serial.print(" Temp = ");
  Serial.print(temp);
  Serial.println(" *C");
  lcd.clear();
  lcd.print("Temperature");
  lcd.setCursor(0,1);
  lcd.print(temp);
  lcd.write((byte)0);
  lcd.print("C");
  delay(400);
}
void gyroShow()
{
 //lcd.setCursor(0,0);
 lcd.clear();
 lcd.print("X   Y   Z");
 Vector rawGyro = mpu.readRawGyro();
 Vector normGyro = mpu.readNormalizeGyro();
 lcd.setCursor(0,1);
 lcd.print(normGyro.XAxis,1);
 lcd.setCursor(6,1);
 lcd.print(normGyro.YAxis,1);
 lcd.setCursor(12,1);
 lcd.print(normGyro.ZAxis,1);
 Serial.print(" Xnorm = ");
 Serial.print(normGyro.XAxis);
 Serial.print(" Ynorm = ");
```

```
Serial.print(normGyro.YAxis);
Serial.print(" Znorm = ");
Serial.println(normGyro.ZAxis);
delay(200);
}
void accelShow()
{
// lcd.setCursor(0,0);
lcd.clear();
lcd.print("X    Y    Z");
Vector rawAccel = mpu.readRawAccel();
Vector normAccel = mpu.readNormalizeAccel();
lcd.setCursor(0,1);
lcd.print(normAccel.XAxis,1);
lcd.setCursor(6,1);
lcd.print(normAccel.YAxis,1);
lcd.setCursor(12,1);
lcd.print(normAccel.ZAxis,1);
Serial.print(" Xnorm = ");
Serial.print(normAccel.XAxis);
Serial.print(" Ynorm = ");
Serial.print(normAccel.YAxis);
Serial.print(" Znorm = ");
Serial.println(normAccel.ZAxis);
delay(200);
}
```